Make-Up, Costumes & Masks for the Stage

by Ole Bruun-Rasmussen and Grete Petersen

Sterling Publishing Co., Inc.   New York

Photographs by Jens Bull

Originally published in Denmark under the titles "Sjove masker af papir"
©1972 by Host & Sons Forlag, Copenhagen, and "Sminkning og maskering"
©1975 by Host & Sons Forlag, Copenhagen. Translated by Kathleen Margaret
Brondal.

Fourth Printing, 1982
Copyright © 1976 by Sterling Publishing Co., Inc.
Two Park Avenue, New York, N.Y. 10016
Distributed in Australia by Oak Tree Press Co., Ltd.
P.O. Box K514 Haymarket, Sydney 2000, N.S.W.
Distributed in the United Kingdom by Blandford Press
Link House, West Street, Poole, Dorset BH15 1LL, England
Distributed in Canada by Oak Tree Press Ltd.
% Canadian Manda Group, 215 Lakeshore Boulevard East
Toronto, Ontario M5A 3W9
Manufactured in the United States of America
All rights reserved
Library of Congress Catalog Card No.: 76-19803
Sterling ISBN 0-8069-7024-3 Trade   Oak Tree 7061-2519-3 Trade
7025-1 Library   2769-2 Paper
8992-0 Paper

Contents

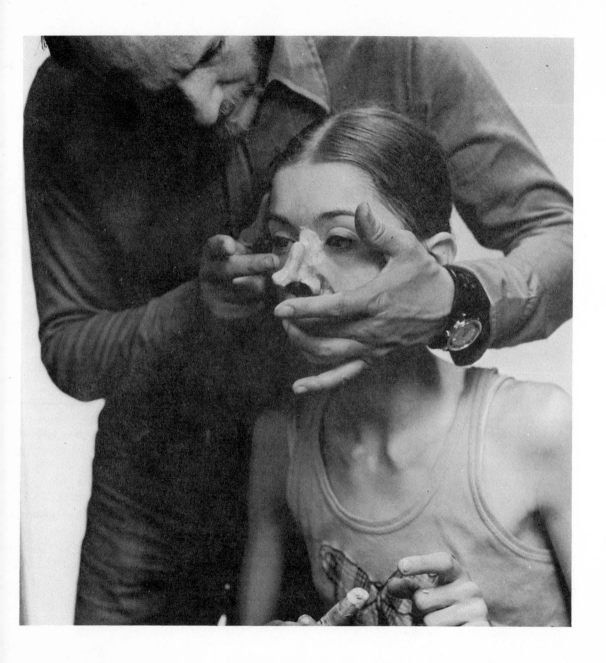

1 Before you begin

Everyone loves a disguise. Little kids "get lost" by holding their hands in front of their faces. Older children become strangers by putting on a special hat. Primitive people disguise themselves when they call for luck in their hunting, or for rain, fertility, victory in war, or whatever they need to survive. In ancient Japan the Samurai used frightening masks to terrorize their enemies; they were part of the warrior's garb. The classical Greeks wore masks when they performed their dramas. Even today in Italy and in many other places, people create giant masks for carnival processions. Masks, of one kind or another, are everywhere.

Children—and grown-ups, too—feel freer when they wear disguises. With a mask you can change your identity and discover completely new unsuspected personalities which are part of yourself. By pretending to be somebody else, you may find something new in yourself which you would never have known about without the mask. That is a large part of what theatre is all about.

This book is meant to start you off exploring all kinds of disguises—make-up itself and quick and easy costumes and comic masks—which you can have fun with at home, at costume parties and masquerades, and even on stage in plays, variety shows and pageants. You can twist a sheet around you and become a Hindu lady, drop the top and turn into a Siamese man, tuck a pillow in your belt and become a buffoon. A putty nose can turn you into a raving witch; a piece of cardboard can make you a villain or a knight. Papier mâché can give you a two-person horse which can (with your help) perform a hilarious act! And it is amazing how little you really need to create an effect!

But don't tie yourself down to these instructions. They will show you how to create an elephant mask, but maybe you'd rather be a tiger, a kangaroo or a yak. With these masks and make-up techniques, you'll be able to create hundreds of animals and people and monsters.

Look around you. The secret of changing your appearance is based on observation. Take as models people you see in the street, on buses and trains, in newspapers. Look for ideas in children's books and at the sketches of anthropologists! It isn't hard to translate them into paper and cloth and grease paint.

Then stand in front of the mirror wearing your new face. You'll discover that your whole body looks different. You've become another person. Your walk changes, your voice, too, and it all happens on its own. You act, play and experiment—you jump right out of everyday life. And while you do it, you learn a few new things about your fellow beings and about yourself.

Have fun!

2 Instant disguises

With a burnt cork

For a quick and simple make-up job, use a blackened cork as your make-up stick. Just burn one end of it with a match. Paint your eyebrows with the cork, and give yourself a couple of lines on your forehead.

To create shadows, draw a line with the cork above each eyelid. Make the line heaviest at your nose and taper it off as it moves outward. Smooth over the soot with your finger, so that the tone moves gradually from dark at your nose and right under your eyebrows to light—almost flesh-colored—at the place where you feel the eye socket and finish off at the hard bone.

You can also use cork for making a moustache. Paint a series of vertical lines under your nose. Continue them the entire width of your mouth and you have a Groucho Marx-type moustache. Did you know that his movie moustaches were painted on?

Complete the disguise with a hat, shirt and tie, together with a pair of long, turned-up pants and perhaps a huge jacket or overcoat. A large pair of shoes, a cigar in one hand, walking stick in the other, and the picture is complete.

With ordinary cosmetics—for girls

If you want to experiment with everyday make-up, first blacken your eyebrows with the burnt cork. Then paint your lips with lipstick. After that, rub a little cold cream into your cheeks, chin and neck, and apply ordinary face powder with a powder puff to your whole face and neck.

Add a few discarded grown-up clothes, high heels and a purse.

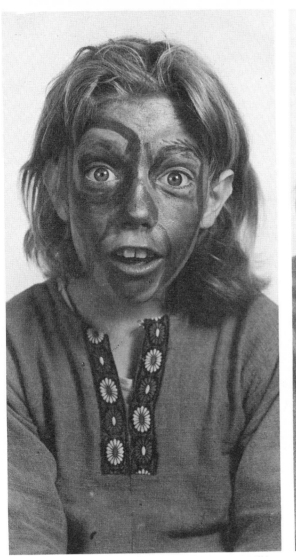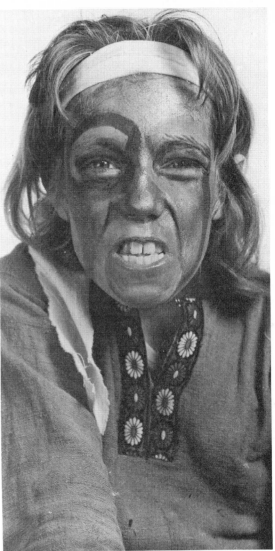

While you make yourself up, help the mask along by making faces. When you find an interesting expression, emphasize it with line and shadow.

With a sheet

With just a sheet, some old clothes and a minimum of make-up, you can create many quick and easy disguises. Most of the very simple ones are based on the "foreign" costumes you see in old-fashioned textbooks. Naturally, you don't want to make fun of other peoples' ways of dressing, but it would be a shame to get so over-sensitive that you don't even play cowboys and Indians anymore!

A ghost

A ghost is an easy thing to start off with and, hopefully, it won't embarrass any living ghost! You need a large sheet which has been discarded, scissors, and a black soft-tip marker.

Pull the sheet over your head and gently put marks on it to outline your eye sockets. Then remove the sheet and cut out holes for the eyes. With the marker, draw a ring around each eye socket and below it, a cross or grinning mouth.

An Arab woman

Cut a square hole in a sheet as shown in the drawing. Then cut two openings for your hands. With one or more colored markers, draw a pattern around the square hole and then place a piece of black net on the upper edge (you can sew it on or stick it on with textile glue), so that it hangs down and covers the whole square. Make-up is not necessary.

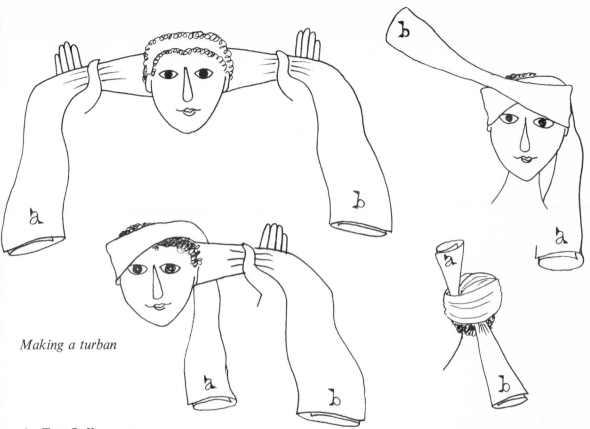

Making a turban

An East Indian man

A traditional Indian costume calls for a turban, and you can make one from a single bed sheet:

1. Fold the sheet together lengthwise twice and hold it as shown in the first drawing.
2. Pass the end marked "a" in front of your forehead and around to the back of your neck—on top of "b"—as shown in the second drawing.
3. See the third drawing. Wind "b" the opposite way around your head twice. Now "b" is hanging down between hair and binding at the back of your neck, while "a" is still loose and sticking out.
4. Spread out "a" and distribute it so that it covers the top of your head.
5. Tuck "a" down at the back of your neck.

Paint a red spot on your forehead, draw heavier eyebrows with the burnt cork, and give yourself a beard if you want to.

For your costume, wear a suit, white shirt and tie.

9

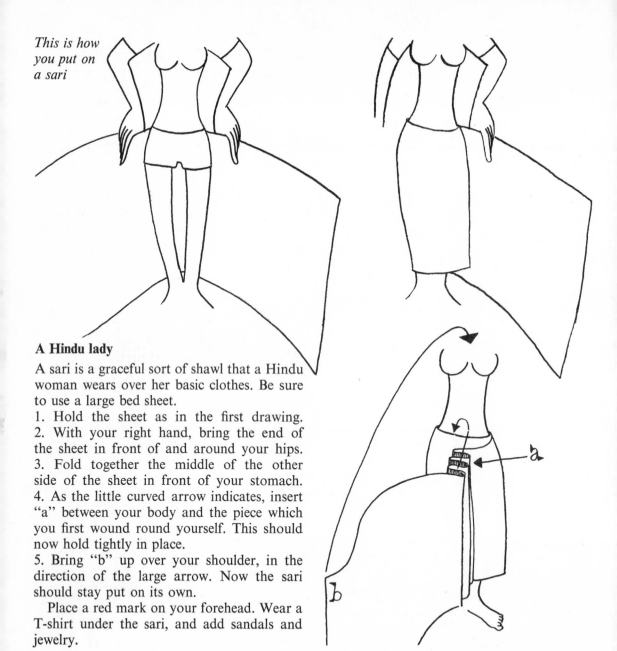

This is how you put on a sari

A Hindu lady

A sari is a graceful sort of shawl that a Hindu woman wears over her basic clothes. Be sure to use a large bed sheet.

1. Hold the sheet as in the first drawing.
2. With your right hand, bring the end of the sheet in front of and around your hips.
3. Fold together the middle of the other side of the sheet in front of your stomach.
4. As the little curved arrow indicates, insert "a" between your body and the piece which you first wound round yourself. This should now hold tightly in place.
5. Bring "b" up over your shoulder, in the direction of the large arrow. Now the sari should stay put on its own.

Place a red mark on your forehead. Wear a T-shirt under the sari, and add sandals and jewelry.

*This is how you
make dhoties*

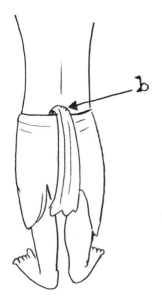

For masquerades, costume parties and Halloween

Hula dancer

Little kids, especially, love to wear grass skirts and flower-bras. Make a grass skirt by tying bunches of straw close together on a string or a clothesline.

For the bra, draw large flowers on cardboard, paint them with bright colors and cut them out. Then string them on a piece of elastic, as shown in the drawing.

Hula skirt

*Flower-bra
for the hula costume*

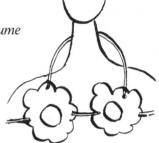

Siamese man

Dhoties are a kind of trousers worn in Siam. You can make them almost exactly as you make the sari. Follow the first four steps. Then put the long end "b" through your legs and up to your back, where you tuck it in between your waist and the material.

Old-fashioned Chinese coolie

Make the coolie hat of thick cardboard. You need scissors, glue and some string.

1. Cut a slice from a round piece of cardboard so that when you bring the sides together, the hat is the size you want (see drawing).
2. Draw the line "a-b" to guide you as you glue the flaps together.
3. Prick 2 holes at "c" as shown in the second drawing.

You could also make a twirled moustache of black wool. Glue it on with spirit gum or make a hanging moustache of crepe hair (see page 46). Of course, you can always paint on a moustache or beard with burnt cork.

This girl made her eyes more Oriental with some strokes of an eyebrow pencil. Her moustache is crepe hair; a braid is glued in her hat. All she needs is a kimono.

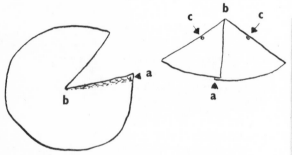

4. Pull a string through the holes from the inside.
5. At each end of the string, which is now on the outside, tie a knot which is big enough so that it won't slip back through the hole.
6. Make a thick braid of black yarn and glue it inside the hat.

For your costume, use a kimono or a loose-hanging jacket and wide pants.

Paint your face pale yellow with a grease paint stick or with body make-up (see page 32). Smooth the make-up with your fingers. Touch up your eyebrows with black grease paint, your lips with red.

Chimney sweep

If you have some black clothes, it is easy to become a chimney sweep. Wear a top hat (see page 72) or a little round felt cap and old sneakers, blackened with cork.

Apply "soot" to your face a little unevenly with the cork so that you can see your skin through it. Don't forget to blacken your hands. Add a little lipstick and perhaps a small moustache.

Bank robber

You will be unrecognizable with a cut-off nylon stocking pulled down over your face. Wear a pair of gloves, and if you don't have any other weapons, carry a section of old pipe. You need a hat and a briefcase to carry off the money. Bring along a pair of sunglasses, so that you will still be incognito when you get tired of wearing the stocking.

Disguising your body

You can create marvelous effects by padding your body.

A fat stomach

Put a small cushion beneath your clothes. To keep it firmly in place, sew cords or tapes onto it. See the drawing.

A cowboy

You probably already have a pair of jeans. Find a wide-brimmed hat (an old soft felt hat is fine), a checkered shirt and a toy pistol for your belt, and coil some clothesline over your shoulder for a lasso. Then, with blue or black grease paint, draw the shadow of whiskers all over your chin.

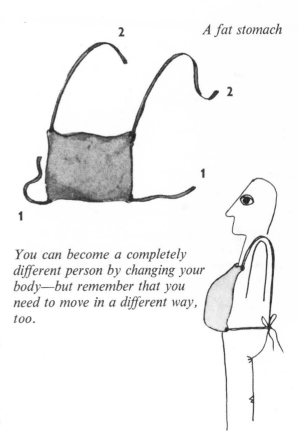

A fat stomach

2

2

1

1

You can become a completely different person by changing your body—but remember that you need to move in a different way, too.

A big bust

You can make falsies from a couple of small plastic cups with handles. Connect the cups with a string tied to the handles. See the drawing.

A large behind

Place one (or more) small cushions inside your clothes. You probably won't need tapes or cords to hold them.

Bumps and lumps and muscles

For a troll or witch costume, you might want bumps and other growths on your elbows, knees, or other parts of your body. Wear something tight, like a leotard or tights. Then insert small pieces of foam rubber wherever you want your lumps. If you want to put them on your arms, use nylon stockings (with the feet cut off) as sleeves. Then glue the lumps to your skin underneath with spirit gum (see page 94). If you're wearing something transparent, make sure the padding is the same color as your outfit.

Use foam rubber to create the super-muscles of a weight-lifter, especially if your own muscles are a little soft.

3 Costume tricks

With a scarf

To change your appearance drastically without much effort, tie a scarf around your head. Here are a number of ways to do it:

Experiment #1: Use a triangular scarf or an ordinary large square. Fold it in half diagonally. Put it on your head so that the corner "c" (see drawing) sticks out in back. Now just make a knot of "a" and "b" under your chin.

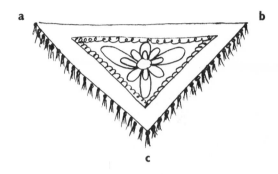

Experiment #2: Using the same scarf, put it over your head so that point "c" sticks out in back. Then bring "a" and "b" around to the back of your neck and tie them together in a knot underneath "c." Let the corner "c" hang down loose at the back.

Experiment #3: Using the same scarf, put it on the top of your head with "c" sticking out over your forehead. Then tie "a" and "b" together in a knot on your forehead across "c." Now pull "c" over the knot and tuck it down between the knot and your forehead. Anchor it with bobby pins.

Experiment #4: You can also use a long, narrow scarf here. Hold it in front of your forehead. Bring the ends to the back of your head, cross them, bring them forward again to your forehead and knot them there.

With a shawl

Experiment #1: Put the shawl over your shoulders with point "c" hanging down behind. Let it hang down loose over your shoulders and keep it together with your hands or with a loose knot tied in front.

Experiment #2: Put the shawl over your shoulders in the same way as before. Cross points "a" and "b" in front of your chest, and pass them under each arm around towards your back. Finally tie them together under "c."

15

Pants legs

You can make particularly wide pants legs for an ordinary pair of pants from a fabric "funnel," sewn with a hem (or casing) at the top and bottom.

1. Cut out a piece of material as shown in the drawing.
2. Sew the two casings first.
3. Sew the funnel together, but don't sew it up all the way to the edges. You need to leave the casings open so that you can slip wire and string through them.

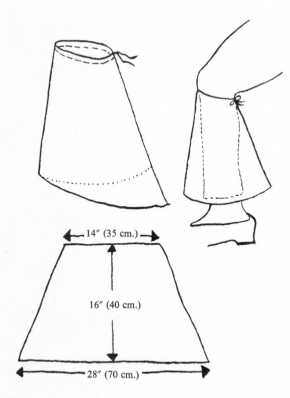

14″ (35 cm.)

16″ (40 cm.)

28″ (70 cm.)

4. Pull a piece of wire through the bottom casing. This will make the pants legs stand out around your ankles.
5. Pull a piece of string or elastic through the top casings, so that you can tie the pants legs on.
6. Tie the pants legs under your knees on top of your real pants so that they cover with a little to spare.

You can make the pants legs of any color, depending on what material you have and the effect you're after.

Jewelry

Jewelry is important to some costumes and you can make effective pieces yourself quite easily. Brass foil and silver foil look like gold and silver ornaments, and you can decorate them with "precious stones" made from pieces of cut glass or beads.

Royal crown

A royal crown consists of an embossed metal foil band with a row of points

*A royal crown
made from metal foil*

as shown in the drawing below. Start your crown by making a paper pattern.

1. Cut a strip of paper approximately an inch (2 cm.) wide. It must be long enough to reach around your head.
2. Cut a number of pointed "leaves" from paper.
3. Attach the leaves to the paper strip with tape and your pattern is ready.
4. Put the resulting pattern on top of a piece of metal foil (see page 94), and with a needle or an awl, carefully scratch in the outline of the pattern.
5. Cut out the crown from the foil with scissors, following your outline.
6. Using a piece of cardboard as an underlay, draw a design into the metal foil with a blunt instrument, such as the crochet hook shown in the drawing. You are "embossing" the leaves. Press hard so that you push the metal down into the cardboard underlay. As you do this, the indentations become raised points on the other side. Finish your embossing process.

7. Turn the metal foil over. Glue the foil, raised points facing you, to a cardboard strip you have cut to the same size as the band. The cardboard will act as a headband to help you wear the crown.
8. Prick 3 holes at each end of the cardboard-strip headband, perforating the outside foil. Now sew the ends together with needle and thread. Your crown is ready to wear!

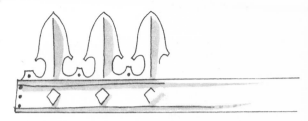

9. For an especially rich crown, paste on some sparkling buttons or glass beads with epoxy glue.

Emboss the metal foil with a crochet hook

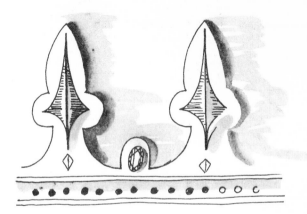

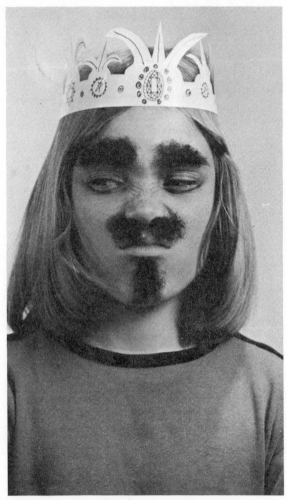

10. Prick a couple of holes on each side of the crown, through which you can stick hairpins to keep it firmly on your head.

You can make other ornaments from metal foil, too, using the same techniques.

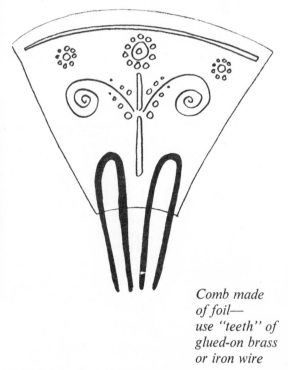

A royal crown doesn't have to break the royal bank. This fierce medieval ruler is wearing a cardboard crown. You make it the same way you make the metal foil crown, but skip the embossing process. His jewels were made with a marker. His whiskers are artificial, too, made of crepe hair.

Comb made of foil— use "teeth" of glued-on brass or iron wire

Fabric or leather bracelet

A simple band can become an elegant ornament with metal foil cutouts "embossed" like the crown and sewn onto the bracelet. You need to cut holes in the leather with a belt-punch where you intend to sew the foil on. Then cut two holes for sewing in each corner of the metal foil cutouts to match the holes in the leather. After you sew the foil on, glue beads onto the foil.

You can decorate belts the same way.

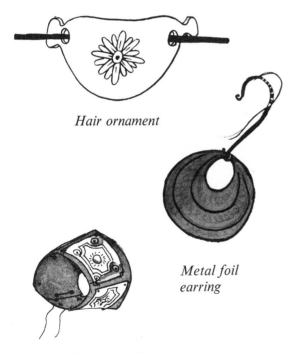

Hair ornament

Metal foil earring

Bracelet with sewn-on foil

Weird wigs

These are comic wigs for masquerades, circus clowns and even some plays. You can make them from almost anything. First, you need some kind of wig foundation, a cap, a stretchy sock, the top of an old hat, a piece of cardboard or cloth—even, if you want to get fancy, a bald head (home-made)—and go on from there! Here's how:

Stringy wig

1. Tie strips of straw onto lengths of string. Cut the straw to whatever length you want.
2. Cut a small, thin circle of cardboard to use as the foundation for the wig. The cardboard should be small enough to fit naturally on the top of your head.
3. Paint the cardboard with flesh-colored poster paint.
4. With a synthetic resin glue (see page 94), paste the straw to the cardboard circle, as shown in the drawing.
5. Spread the straw so that the cardboard is hidden and keep the wig in place by putting hairpins through the cardboard into your real hair.

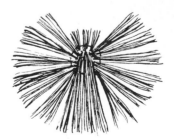

This wig is made of straw, with each individual strand sewn onto the crown of a hat. Natural straw was used here, but you can use colored braiding straw for unusual effects.

You can create a funny wig by attaching cotton string or twine directly to your real hair with bobby pins. Arrange the hairdo with your fingers; a comb will only rip it up and a brush will stick.

Hair color

If you want to color the hair you're using, dye it before you glue it on with ordinary cold dye or stain. Then spread diluted glue on the wig foundation with a thin paintbrush and stick the hair on.

Cloth wig foundation

You can use a piece of round cloth as a wig foundation, too. Sew darts at the edge of the cloth until it fits your head.

Putting hair on your wig

An easy way to cut the "hair" is to wind the strands of whatever you're using around a piece of cardboard or a book. Cut it, as shown in the drawing. Now you have several strands of hair which are equal lengths.

More wigs

You can also glue, sew or staple scraps of yarn, excelsior (the strips of paper that glass is packed in) or absorbent cotton (cotton wool) onto a piece of cardboard. Whatever you use, spread the "hair" with your fingers so that it covers the foundation, and anchor the wig with hairpins.

Cut the hair

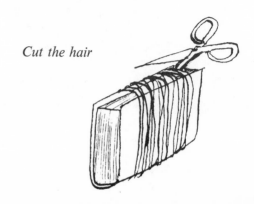

The most simple method of making a long-haired wig is to sew the hair along the edge of the wig foundation and continue around it in layers, making the hair as thick as you want (see drawing).

If you want a wig with braids, sew the hair onto the cloth in the center to make a "natural" part (see drawing).

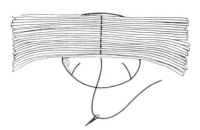

If your foundation is a cap or the crown of an old hat, you might want to try this method with the "cut" hair:

1. Cut some pieces of fabric tape, long enough (approximately) to encircle the cap.
2. Either sew one end of the cut-up strands of hair to a piece of tape, or double them over if you prefer as shown in the drawing. Prepare several of these hair-tapes at the same time.

*Sew the hair
to a piece
of tape*

3. Pin the hair-tapes to the cap, starting at the bottom and working your way around. As soon as one piece of tape reaches around, sew it onto the cap. Then again, pin and sew, layer upon layer. When you reach the crown of the cap, and one last hole is left uncovered, complete the fastening with a piece of tape which has an equal length of material on each end.
4. Arrange the hairdo with your fingers. As with the other weird wigs, don't use a comb or brush.

Bald head

You can use the bald head plain, or you can paste hair onto part or all of it (see the clowns on page 76). The bald head is actually a wig foundation of its own, made out of gauze mâché, a paste and gauze concoction which is like papier mâché but lighter and more pliable. Use ordinary gauze that you buy at the supermarket or pharmacy.

Gauze maché technique

1. Cut the gauze into small pieces—about 2 inches (5 cm.) square—and put them in a row, ready to use.
2. Dilute a synthetic resin glue (see page 94) according to the printed instructions. The diluted paste should not be too runny.
3. Use a blown-up balloon as the base for the gauze mâché. Place the balloon in a container to hold it steady while you work. With a tape-measure or a piece of string, make sure that the balloon corresponds to the outline of your head.
4. With a brush approximately $1\frac{1}{2}$ inches (3 cm.) wide, and wet with glue, pick up one piece of gauze at a time and paste it down on top of the balloon, each piece overlapping the previous one, and smooth it out.
5. Don't worry about making the edges perfect. You can cut the bald head later into the shape you want.
6. Apply 2 or 3 layers of gluey gauze to the balloon. If you don't like the clothlike surface, glue on a layer of tissue paper torn into small shreds.
7. Let it dry overnight.
8. Cut it to size.

To keep the bald head on, insert a thin elastic from ear to ear and at the back of the neck (see drawing). Do this *before* the mâché is dry or it will be too hard to puncture.

Paint the head with flesh-colored poster paint.

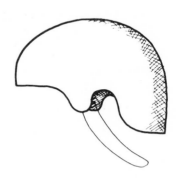

Disguising your face

Spectacles

You can cut spectacles from paper or cardboard, but they are far more realistic when you make them out of wire.

1. Cut 2 pieces of lightweight wire approximately 18 inches (45 cm.) each.
2. Using your fingers, shape one end of each wire into a circle.
3. Attach the 2 wire circles in the middle by twisting a third, small piece of wire about $\frac{1}{2}$ inch (1.25 cm.) long between and around the circles. This forms the bridge of the spectacles.

4. Shape the ends of the original wires into side bars. They should be long enough to reach down around your ears (see drawing 1).

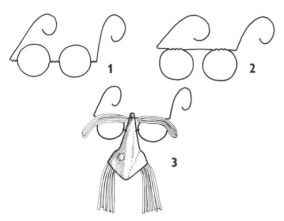

You can also make a pair of glasses from just one piece of wire (see drawing 2), and equip it with nose and eyebrows.

Nose disguise

The distinguished nose in drawing 3 is made of gauze mâché (see page 22) over a bit of sheet metal. You keep it together with tape.

Did you notice the wart on one side? Make it by gluing a small wad of paper or half a pea between the layers of gauze.

Paint the nose with poster paint and sew or glue it onto the glasses.

Add grey yarn for the bushy eyebrows and beard. Glue or sew them onto the glasses and nose.

Nose and cheek set

In the photograph, the girl's cheeks are made of gauze mâché over 2 halves of a small rubber ball.

1. Grease the ball with petroleum jelly.
2. Cover the ball with gauze mâché.
3. When the ball is dry, give it a coat of flesh-colored paint with a rosy glow.
4. Draw a line around the middle of the ball and carefully cut it in half with a craft knife.
5. Make the nose from stiff paper shaped like a cone; better still, use the bottom of a cone-shaped paper cup.
6. Strengthen it with tape on the inside edge.
7. Prick 2 holes in each of the 3 parts and run through a thin piece of elastic from the nose (see drawing 5). For even sturdier nose and cheeks, glue the three parts together with fabric tape before inserting the elastic.

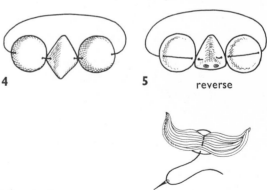

Moustache

If you find it difficult to keep a moustache together, sew the hair onto a little piece of cloth and keep it in shape with a brushing of diluted glue or a coating of egg white.

A handsome couple! The lady wears a nose and cheek set, the gent—a nose disguise made out of papier mâché, wire and yarn.

4 Using make-up

Your make-up kit might be a tool box which is available in several sizes.

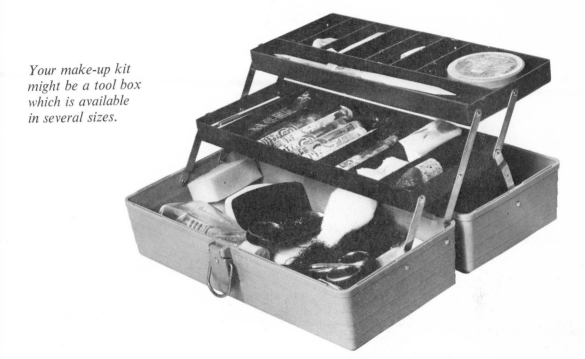

The make-up kit

It's a good idea to keep all your make-up supplies in one place. Many actors and actresses use a tool box, the kind you buy at a hardware store. What goes into it depends on your needs. In the kit in the photograph, you'll find the make-up you need to create this book's cast of characters.

Basic equipment

Cork and matches
Eyebrow pencil
Hand mirror
Comb
Cleansing cream
Scissors (pointed)

Soft-tip marker (Never use a marker for making up your face. You may be allergic to it and it's difficult to remove.)
Grease paint sticks
Craft knife blade
Fur or crepe hair (for making beards and hair)
Spirit gum (glue in a bottle)
Spirit gum remover (or rubbing alcohol, but spirit gum remover is likely to be less harsh to your skin)
Nose putty
Stage powder
Powder puff
Eye shadow
Olive oil or moisture cream (if your skin is sensitive)
Brushes, with pointed tips (the kind artists use)

Along with your make-up kit, but not in it, you need:
Towel (for cleaning your fingers after you blend your make-up)
Tissues

Unlikely equipment for a make-up kit? Not at all!

Choosing grease paint sticks

Grease paint sticks are made for painting directly on your skin, the same way you use a brush or pencil. Softer than oil pastel crayons and rather greasy, the sticks measure about 4 inches (10 cm.) long. They are fairly expensive, but they last a long time, especially if you have several sticks and mix your colors. You don't have to store them in any special way because they don't dry up.

An immense range of colors is available, but you don't need to buy a large selection all at once. Build up your collection gradually, filling in as you need different colors. The supplier list on page 95 includes several manufacturers who print catalogues and will send them to you if you write for a copy. Take a look at the chart on page 38. It will help you to decide what grease paint sticks you need and what colors to use for each purpose.

Preparing for make-up

Before you start making up, there are a few things you ought to do.
1. Set yourself up comfortably in front of a fixed mirror, with your make-up next to you.
2. See to it that light shines down on you from above. That will produce the same effect as natural daylight and you will be able to see how the shadows fall on your face. This is particularly important if you are making up for the stage. If the light falls on your face from all sides, it is even better, since stage lighting comes from many different places. If you have an adjustable lamp, one that turns in all directions, use it. Read "Stage light and shadow" on page 36 before you begin.

3. Keep a small hand mirror within reach. You need to see your face at close quarters.
4. Wash your face *before* making up and rinse it in cold water. The water will close the pores of your skin. Men should be freshly shaven.
5. Protect your clothes by wearing an old shirt or robe.
6. Spread a towel over your lap.
7. Protect your hair with a cap or scarf.
8. Have a smaller towel and some tissues handy so that you can clean your fingers after you rub on the make-up.

Experimenting with make-up

Take two pieces of candy (about the size of marbles) in your mouth—don't swallow them. Roll them into your cheeks so that you get two bumps. Then take a black grease paint stick and draw a ring around each bump. Use the stick in the same way that you use a brush or pencil.

Take the candy out and fill in the circles with black. Look in the mirror again.

Look at the drawing on this page and make similar experiments yourself, but only with the black color. Use your imagination. See how many possibilities there really are, even with just one color.

When you finish your first painting experiments, look into the mirror. Squint at your reflection until it becomes a bit blurred. Doing this, you get an impression of how your make-up looks from a distance.

In your next experiments, use two colors. Remember to squint to get an idea of how your make-up will look when you're on stage.

In your third series of experiments, look at your face as two identical halves and really let yourself go. Use all the make-up colors you have.

Finally, try to repeat the face you liked best. But this time, paint the nose a bright red, and make the mouth large and crooked. It won't be long now before you create a classic circus mask.

Make-up experiments with one color

The great clown masks

The white clown

With a white grease paint stick, draw thick lines all over your face except for your eyebrows and lips. Remember to make your neck white, too. Rub in the white color with your fingers so that it covers evenly.

With a black eyebrow pencil, draw one large eyebrow, as shown on the drawing, and add a beauty spot on one cheek. Paint your lips with a bright red grease paint stick, your ears with a lighter red color.

The white clown always wears a thick crop of hair, which has been plastered down with water, and a cone-shaped hat you can make yourself in a minute. Cut a piece of cardboard, as shown on page 29. Remember that the head measurement has to correspond to "a," making an overlapping edge, so that you can glue the hat together.

The white clown wears a white, tight-fitting jacket covered with a mass of spangles. Spangles are available already sewn together on long pieces of tape. Cut the tapes into the lengths you need and sew them on in whatever patterns you choose.

It is not easy to sew the wide, jodhpur pants, so use plain white pajama pants, instead. Wear white shoes (sneakers will do) and stockings.

Another classic part of the white clown's outfit is the white-painted cane with a white bag tied on the end. The bag contains rice kernels. The clown uses it to punish his friend, "The Buffoon."

Clown masks are always stylized. Quickly and simply they tell us something about what the clown is like—boisterous or sad, mischievous or lazy.

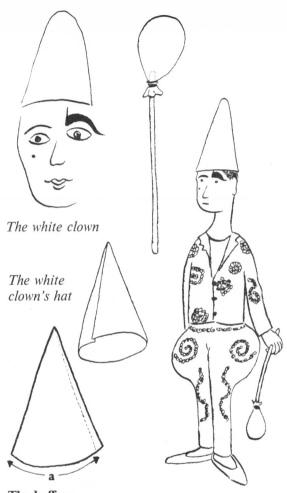

The white clown

The white clown's hat

a

The buffoon

With a pale purple grease paint stick, paint lines all over your face and neck, except for your nose. Blend the color with your fingers. Emphasize your eyebrows with a yellowish-brown stick. On top of the pale purple base color, draw half-moon-shaped eyebags with a green stick. Paint your nose and mouth vivid

A floor mop makes a stubborn dog, but the buffoon is optimistic. He thinks it might be possible to get the dog to walk, if he pulls hard enough.

red. The lines between each color must be distinct.

If you don't want to bother with a wig, let your own hair bristle out from beneath a hat or cap.

Wear a wide-striped T-shirt, much too wide pants with suspenders and a large jacket. You can keep the pants away from your body by pulling a piece of wire through the inside top seam. Wear two odd shoes or galoshes.

The classical clown

This clown has cross-shaped eyes, as shown in the drawing. His nose is round and red. His mouth is large and it goes right up his cheeks; choose the color yourself. His hair stands on end. You can make him a wig of straw or woollen yarn (see page 19) and spray it with plenty of hair spray to stiffen it.

A tiny derby sits on the clown's head. You can make it any size you want.

To make the derby:

1. Use a blown-up balloon as the base for your construction. Blow it up just enough so that the top of it is the size you want for the crown of your derby.

2. Follow the instructions for gauze mâché on page 22.

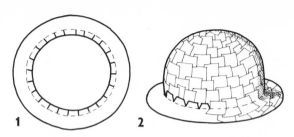

3. When the derby is dry, cut it straight at the edge.
4. Cut a cardboard brim and glue it onto the crown with more gauze (see drawing 2).
5. Glue a strip of paper around the brim as a hatband.
6. If the hat is too large, put a "sweatband" inside the hat (one or more strips of paper or cardboard glued on) until it is the size you want.
7. When the hat is dry, paint it with poster paints.

The classical clown always wears clothes that are much too large. Give him an oversized shirt or a nightshirt on which you've painted cross-stripes in bright colors with a flat paint-brush. Use water-soluble stain for the stripes, and just follow the instructions on the package. Put newspapers inside the shirt before you use the stain because it goes right through the material. If you can get hold of an old, discarded tuxedo—or tails—you could wear them instead. Just remember that all the clothes must be too large, including shoes.

See page 75 for more modern clowns.

5 Stage make-up

Foundation

If you want to look natural on stage, choose a grease paint that will give you a good tan. If you need to look old and worn, apply a greenish-yellow stick. If you are playing a character who spends a great deal of time out-of-doors, you may want to look "flushed." If you are playing a slightly tipsy character, use a reddish tone with a violet tinge.

To apply foundation make-up, start off by drawing some thick lines with the grease paint stick. You need two lines on your forehead, one on each cheek, one on your chin, and two on your neck, as shown in the drawing.

Now, with your fingers and palms, spread the color so that the make-up covers fairly evenly. Then pat your face with your fingers so that the color becomes completely smooth. See to it that the make-up goes all the way up to your hairline and all the way down to a little below your collar.

Don't forget your ears. They need the same color. Here, too, smooth out the color with your fingers.

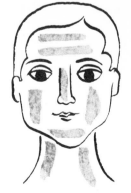

Foundation make-up before you smooth it over your skin

Body make-up

If you need to use make-up all over your body, or on a large part of it, in order to become an Indian brave, for example, use liquid make-up. You can buy it in bottles in stores that sell make-up, and it is ready to use.

Apply liquid make-up with a small piece of absorbent cotton (cotton wool). After you've covered your skin, rub the make-up smooth with dry palms. Continue rubbing and "polishing" until no rims or stripes show. You can't cover blemishes by applying more make-up. The only thing to do is rub and smooth them out.

Liquid make-up is easy to remove. Just take a bath or wash thoroughly with soap and water. Use only a little water and plenty of soap; a rich lather cleans better. Finally, rinse well with water to get rid of all the soap.

Adding definition

To add shadows to your face, spread a light brown grease paint in your eye sockets and on your eyelids. Smooth it out with your fingers, so that the dark color gradually tapers off down the sides of your nose (but not on the ridge of it). Remember that your fingers must be clean every time you start smoothing out the color.

Spread rouge (Crimson red, for example) on your cheekbones, and only there. See the drawing. Blend in the color with your fingers so that the color transition is smooth.

Males, especially if they are dark-haired, should dab an ordinary blue color carefully on the chin. It should be just a mere hint of a growth of beard.

Your basic work is almost finished, but your face is too shiny for the glaring stage lights. Powder it (cover your hair while you do it) with a large powder puff and don't be stingy. You can brush away extra powder with a bit of absorbent cotton (cotton wool). If you have applied the powder correctly, your face will look dry and non-greasy.

*Use red on
your cheekbones only*

32

The finer work

Your eyes

First, touch up your eyebrows. The color you use depends on your hair color. If you want to look dark-haired, paint your eyebrows black. If you are playing a fair-haired person, use a chestnut-brown.

Dip a small artist's brush (the kind that comes to a point) into one end of the oily grease paint stick (see drawing). You will use this brush to touch up your eyebrows and to outline your eyes. Start towards the root of your nose and brush outwards with the hairs.

Then, at the bottom of your eyelids and just above the lashes, draw a very thin line with the same color. Do the same thing just below your bottom eyelashes, outlining your eyes, as shown in the drawing.

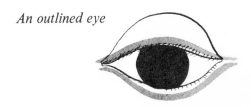

An outlined eye

To make your eyes look much larger, simply draw the outlines a little farther away from your eyes.

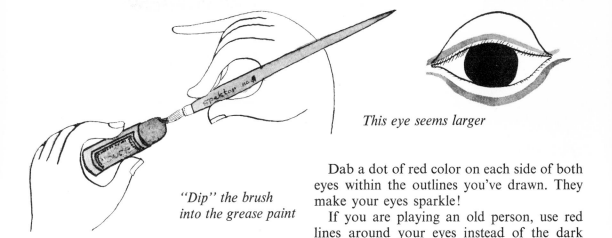

"Dip" the brush into the grease paint

This eye seems larger

Dab a dot of red color on each side of both eyes within the outlines you've drawn. They make your eyes sparkle!

If you are playing an old person, use red lines around your eyes instead of the dark color. As people age, their eyes often appear smaller, so keep the red lines close to your eyelashes.

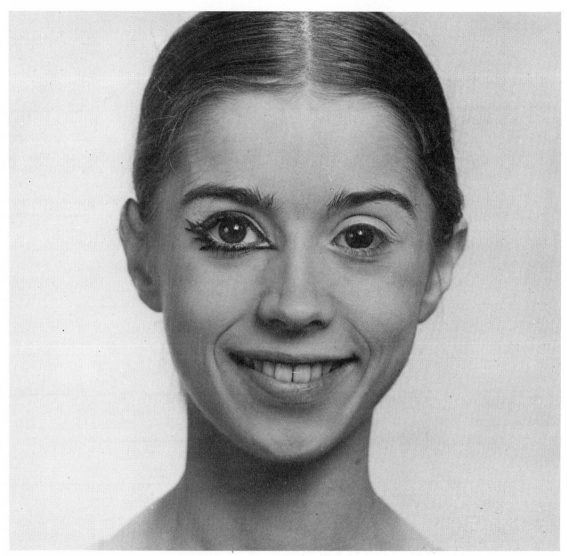

Only half of this girl's face has been made-up. Cover that half with a piece of paper. Then switch the paper. The made-up half stands out clearly, even at a fairly long distance. If you hold a pocket mirror vertically through the middle of her face, you'll see what the girl looks like when she is completely made-up.'

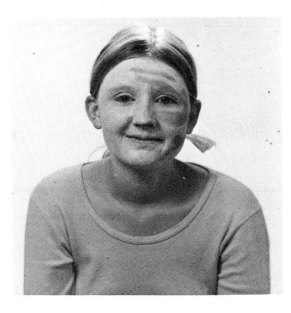

Your mouth

Touch up your lips, but be careful not to use too much color. Too much lip rouge looks unnatural. Don't use ordinary lipstick; it shines too much under stage lighting. Besides, it is not so easy to get it off. It is better to use red-orange grease paint.

If you want your lower lip to jut out, make it a little lighter than your upper lip.

To make your lower lip look larger, paint your upper lip slightly smaller than it actually is and your lower lip a little larger. If your lower lip is just a couple of hairlines fuller than normal, it will show up well. Carry out this delicate work as accurately as you can. You need to apply the color very carefully to make it look smooth and natural. Make-up only "works" when you don't look made-up!

A young girl transforms herself into a sour, grumpy old woman. Her dropped shoulder-line and black dress with white trim add to the general effect.

Stage light and shadow

To get the best results with your make-up, you need to know about the play of light and shadow. In contrast to daylight and ordinary overhead light, stage lighting blurs the lines of your face, and it is these lines or contours which you need to re-define.

How shadows work

Look at the photograph on the left below: A lamp is shining on a ball which has been cut in half. The light hits the ball diagonally from above and lights up the inside of the ball. The lower part of the inside is lit up; the upper part is in shadow.

The human face has parts which are curved in and out like the surface of a ball.

Now look at the other photograph. When you turn the ball over, so that the outside is lit up, the upper part of the ball is lighted and the lower part is in shadow.

If you want to look apple-cheeked, you would make up lighter towards the top of your cheekbone and darker at the bottom.

Hollow cheek

Apple cheek

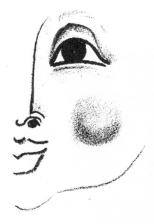

When you look at facial features, you can compare their light and shadow with that of the ball. In the drawing with the hollow cheek, light hits the face in the same way it did on the left half of the ball. The upper part of the "inside" is in shadow.

The drawing with the apple cheek is like the other half of the ball. Here the upper part is light and the lower one is darker.

The ball helps you see what you have to color a little darker if you want to look hollow-cheeked: the upper part of the "inside"; in other words, the area around the eye and below the cheekbone, as shown in the hollow-cheek drawing.

The light on the ball comes from above because that is the way it falls naturally in daylight and also on stage.

You won't go wrong if you remember that where the real, natural shadows fall, you need the darker shadings. You shade deep-set eyes, but light protruding ones; you darken the sharp bridge of the nose and light the turned-up one; light the prominent chin and prominent cheekbone, but darken sunken cheeks.

Rôle	Foundation	Cheeks	Definition for Eye shadow	Wrinkles	Lips	Other features
Fair-haired girl or lady	fair skin	red	dark brown	brown	red	—
Fair-haired boy or man	fair skin	dark skin	brown	brown	faint carmine	beard—use with foundation blue or greyish blue on chin
Medium-blonde girl or lady	fair/medium-colored skin	carmine	bluish grey	brown	carmine	—
Dark-haired girl or lady	medium-colored skin	carmine	dark brown black-brown	brown	carmine	—
Dark-haired boy or man	medium-colored skin	dark skin	brown	black-brown black	—	beard complexion blue or greyish blue
Grey or white haired old lady	medium colored skin	carmine	dark brown	light-grey	carmine	clay for false nose
Grey-haired man	fair skin	medium-colored skin	cream-colored dark brown black-brown	brown	possibly red	clay for false nose
White-haired old man	light yellow skin	carmine	cream-colored dark brown black-brown	brown	pale red (white mixed with red)	clay for false nose

This table is simply a guide to the most common situations and it doesn't take into account specific facts about your character. For example, if the grey-haired man is inclined to drink a bit much, his skin might be reddish or even violet. If the dark-haired young lady has just had some traumatic experience, her skin might be practically grey. Use your own imagination!

This girl is using an adjustable lamp to examine the play of light and shadow. Once she sees how the shadows fall on her face naturally, she can emphasize them with make-up. Also (with some light powder), she can diminish shadows which are in the way.

Character make-up

A false nose

If you want your nose to look larger or to have a different shape, re-shape it with nose putty before you make yourself up. Nose putty is a kind of plasticine clay which does not dry out, so there are no storage problems. (See page 94.)

1. Knead a piece of nose putty in your hands until it becomes soft. If you want it to have a ruddy color, scrape off a little red from a grease paint stick with a knife and mix it into the putty. Knead thoroughly.

2. Press the soft nose putty onto your finger, as shown in the drawing, and model it into the shape you want.

3. When you have the shape right—more or less—take the putty off your finger and press

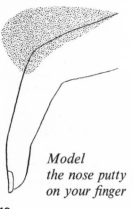

Model the nose putty on your finger

Here and on the next page, you'll see 5 steps in the creation of a witch. Notice how the girl acts the part while she puts on her make-up. She is finding witchy expressions in her own face and emphasizing them.

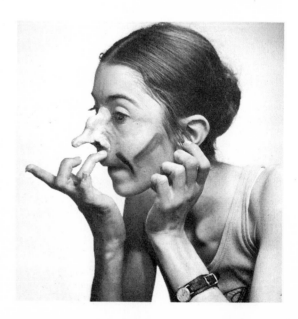

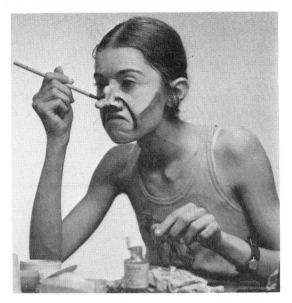

Look at the bottom picture. The witch can become a raving lunatic.

it carefully onto your nose. Make sure that it stays put.

4. Smooth out the putty so that the surface is even and there is no obvious line between the clay and your skin. It helps to dab a little grease—cleansing cream will do—onto your fingertips as you work. If you damaged the nose when you stuck it on, this is the time to correct its shape.

5. When you finish your new nose, start your full make-up job.

It is a sticky job, modelling a nose, but you can do it with a bit of practice, deftness and care.

Ears and Warts

To change the shape of your ear, use nose putty in the same way. You can also conjure up warts and other growths.

Wrinkles

When you paint wrinkles, be particularly careful and remember an important rule: Never make wrinkles where there aren't traces of wrinkles already! The whole purpose of adding wrinkles to your make-up is for them to underline the movements of your face, and "false" wrinkles won't do it.

If you don't have wrinkles yet, try to figure out where they should appear. Talk in front of the mirror. Make faces, smile, frown, squint. You'll be able to tell where the wrinkles should be so that they emphasize the movements of your face.

Never make more wrinkles than you absolutely need. Usually, all you need to do is emphasize the wrinkles around your eyes and the ones at the corners of your mouth.

To create a wrinkle:

1. Draw a line with the tip of a brush (the same kind you used for the lines around your eyes). Use a dark red or dark brown color and draw the line exactly where the wrinkle is—in the "bottom" of the wrinkle.

2. If the wrinkle is deep, make a light stripe beneath the red or brown line. These two colors, one light and the other dark, should lie quite close together.

3. The light color should taper off downwards; the wrinkle should taper off to either side. Taper the dark wrinkle-line by sliding a couple of clean fingers over it carefully, from the middle out to both sides.

Scars

If you're a pirate, you certainly should have a scar.

1. With the tip of your brush, paint a thin red or dark purple line. Taper it with clean fingers.
2. On each side of the red line, paint a thin white stripe. These give the illusion of a very deep scar. (Look at the photograph on page 44).
3. Finally, with the grease paint stick itself, draw red dots like eyelets alongside the scar.

Bags under the eyes

Pirate without make-up. The same boy was a clown on page 29. Look at the natural shadows under his eyes and at his mouth. He will emphasize them with make-up.

Besides a moustache, the pirate has hair on his chest and bushy eyebrows made of crepe hair. He glued his false eyebrows immediately above his real ones. Avoid bushy eyebrows, if you can.

Spirit gum won't hurt your eyes, but it's no fun to get it in them! You can use burnt cork instead. An eyebrow pencil drew the tattoo on his arm. A marker would not have shown up so well and would be more difficult to remove.

43

The pirate's earring is a brass curtain ring; he sawed through it with a coping saw. Then he pulled it open far enough so that it would sit in his ear lobe without hurting. His eye patch is home-made—cardboard, painted black on both sides, with a piece of string. His large snub nose has been shaped with nose putty.

When you finish

When you finish making up, check to be sure that you haven't forgotten to make-up hands, perhaps bare arms, feet, legs, and other parts of your body which show. They must have a basic make-up if you're going to look natural.

How to get the make-up off

When you are ready to remove your make-up, rub a rich cleansing cream over your face. Then remove it with tissues and your make-up will come off. You may need to repeat the process a couple of times.

When you have removed your make-up as well as you can, wash your face thoroughly with soap and water. Use a little water and plenty of soap for best results.

Finally, you may want to put a little moisture cream on your skin so that it doesn't get too dry. You need to be careful about the cleansing operation, especially if you have sensitive skin.

Real wigs

If you want a different hair color, or a completely different hairstyle, you may need to use a ready-made wig, but try doing without it, if you can. Even a slight change in your own hair may create the effect you want. For example, dark-haired people can go grey at the temples by rubbing a little white grease paint into their hair and running a comb through it. You can do the same with your eyebrows and, if you have one, your beard.

Ready-made wigs look natural, but they are expensive to rent or buy. They are also delicate and difficult to handle. Some ready-made wigs are made of human hair, others of synthetic materials. Human hair is better, but artificial hair is cheaper and really very good.

Putting on the wig

Some of the wigs you buy or rent have "forehead skin," especially men's wigs. The forehead skin covers your own hair, and if your wig has it, you need to put the wig on before you apply your make-up.

It is easier to make the wig sit properly if you have someone to help you put it on. You should hold both sides of the wig forehead while your helper pulls the wig firmly down over your head. Make sure that it sits completely straight: the "bits" at the sides should be equal distances from your ears, and the wig should fit snugly all the way round.

Glue it down with spirit gum (see page 94). Spread the liquid on the lower edge of the forehead skin of the wig and also on your own forehead. Then press the wig tightly against your skin for two or three minutes, until the fluid is dry.

If the wig is a little too big, take it in just behind each ear. If it is much too big, don't experiment with it, at least not until an expert has adjusted it.

If your wig doesn't have forehead skin, pin it onto your own hair with hairpins. As a rule, ladies' wigs don't have forehead skin, and you don't put them on until your make-up is complete, but it is a good idea to try on the wig as soon as you can so that you have plenty of time to have it adjusted, if necessary.

It can be difficult to tuck long hair under a wig. Gather your hair at the back of your neck and pile it on top of your head. Hold it in place with a piece of gauze you wrap around your head and fasten at the back of your neck. You can also use the foot of a nylon stocking as a hood to keep your hair close to your head.

Finally, check to make sure that no wisps of your own hair poke out from under the wig.

Beards, whiskers and bushy eyebrows

If you are not satisfied with beards made from burnt cork, you can try working with fur remnants. In shops that sell make-up, you can also buy crepe hair, a braid of artificial hair you can use for making beards, whiskers and bushy eyebrows. It comes in many hair colors. Untie the braid at one end and cut off as much hair as you think you'll need. You will glue the crepe hair directly onto your skin with spirit gum (see page 94).

To calculate the length of crepe hair you want for a beard, figure on a length from your lips to your chin or chest, and cut the hair to that length.

Crepe hair is very curly, so if you want to have a straight beard, you need to smooth out the curls by steaming the hair while you stretch it with both hands to straighten it. Keep the crepe hair stretched out until it cools. If you don't use all of the straightened hair, you can get it to curl a little by steaming it again but only hold one end of the hair.

When you stick on a beard, start at the bottom of your chin and build up the beard in layers, so that each section overlaps the last. If you want a thick beard, glue the pieces of crepe hair close together.

When the beard is glued on, trim it with scissors to the shape you want.

If you want to make a full beard of crepe hair, finish your make-up before you put it on. Spirit gum will not hold the beard, however, if your skin is greasy from make-up or cleansing cream, so you have to clean the places where you are going to place the beard. Use soap and water and perhaps a few drops of rubbing alcohol.

Then dab or paint a little spirit gum onto your clean dry skin, where the beard is to sit. Wait a couple of seconds before you put the beard on—that makes it hold better. Then press the beard to your skin for a few minutes until it holds firmly.

Very large full beards (curly or straight) seldom look natural in crepe hair, especially at close quarters, because it is difficult to make them cover completely. You can rent a ready-made beard, if necessary, from a theatrical costume supplier.

This girl did magic tricks with her long hair. She tied it into a knot and keeps it together with a mass of hairpins. Its shape emphasizes the witch-mask with its pointed nose.

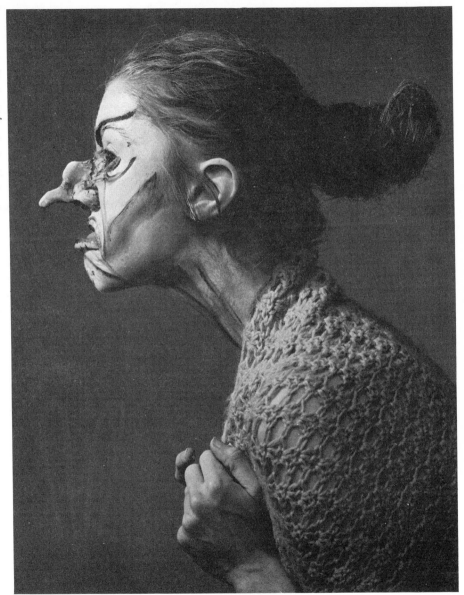

Removing a beard

To remove a beard, pull it off in tufts and take off what is left with spirit gum remover or rubbing alcohol. Then wash your face with soap and water and apply a little moisturizing cream to your skin.

If you still have some spirit gum on your face, remove it with a little piece of absorbent cotton (cotton wool) dipped in spirit gum remover or rubbing alcohol.

There are many ways to make beards.

6 Easy paper masks

From painted masks to paper masks

Paper masks are another kind of make-up, and with them you can create an even more complete disguise. If you are using them on stage, they have several advantages: Make-up can take an hour or more to apply, but once you've made your paper mask, it only takes a moment to put it on. While make-up only transforms your appearance within the limitations of your own facial features, many paper masks totally disguise you. Because masks are so quick to put on and take off, you can change character with miraculous speed. If you are playing several different parts in a melodrama or fantasy, for example, you can step on and off stage as a different person many times in the same show. And if your skin is sensitive, you don't need to bother with make-up at all, and you can still perform.

It doesn't take much time to make a mask. You can put simple paper ones together amazingly fast. Even little children can do it.

You don't need fancy materials, either. Part of the mask game is improvising, and you rarely have to go far for paper and cardboard! Is there a grocery bag within reach? Some wrapping paper, or corrugated cardboard, aluminum foil (kitchen variety)? Even a large cereal box can become a mask—just cut holes for eyes, nose and mouth. Use newspaper for a soldier's hat, with tassels of tissue paper. Add a few old clothes, and you're ready to go.

There are several different types of masks:

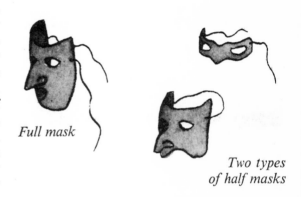

Full mask

Two types of half masks

The full mask

This mask covers your whole face. You'll find many full masks on the following pages.

The half mask

This type covers only part of your face, usually the area around your eyes, but sometimes your nose, too. If you make a half mask, you need a little more color for your face. You can use your eyebrow pencil and grease paint to add character and detail.

Mask patterns

Even simple masks turn out better if you make a pattern before you start making the mask. You can cut the pattern out of wrapping paper or newspaper.

To make a pattern:

1. Start by measuring exact openings for eyes, nose, mouth and ears. Use a regular wax crayon the color of which comes off easily.

2. Hold the pattern paper in front of your face, feel for your eyes and mark them with the crayon (see drawing 1).

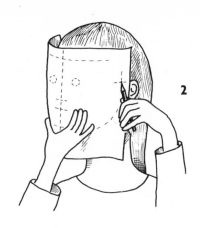

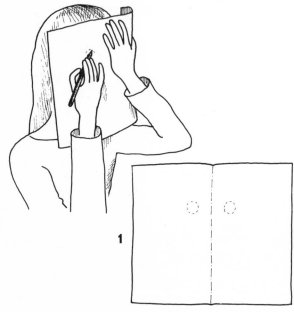

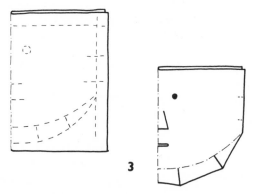

3. Lay the pattern flat and cut holes to look through.

4. Mark nose, mouth and ears. Also indicate the place where you want to fasten an elastic band to the mask, either to go around the back of your head or to tie around your ears.

5. Hold up the pattern again and decide how far up your forehead the mask should go and how far down your chin. If you want it to go down beneath your chin, make one or more cuts in the bottom of it. This makes the mask bend in under your chin and gives it a flexible shape (see drawing 3 on page 50).

6. You can fold the pattern in the middle and cut it double, but you may run into some problems. Not everybody's eyes are set at exactly the same level.

If you cut several masks using the same pattern, remember that they have to be fitted to the people who will be wearing them. Some people's eyes are close together, others are a little further apart. The position of eyes and mouth can vary widely. If you become a mask-maker, you will be amazed at how different two faces can be!

How to strengthen the mask so that the elastic doesn't pull out or rip it: First reinforce the edge of the mask by gluing on a layer of gauze (see page 22). Put the elastic through bits of cardboard and staple or glue them to the inside edge of the mask, as in the drawing.

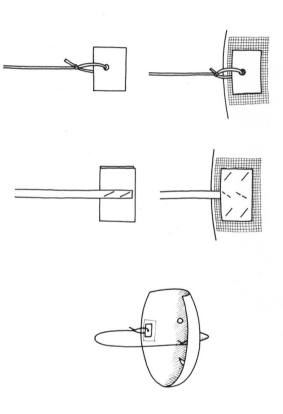

Paper bag masks

You can make the most simple kind of mask from a large paper bag. If the only grocery bag you have has advertising printed on it, carefully turn it inside out. Pull the bag over your head and feel your way to your eyes and mouth. Mark them off with a crayon. Now take the bag off and cut small holes to see through and a small slit for your mouth.

Place the bag flat on the table and paint it with poster paints or whatever you have.

If you want to paint hair on your mask, push in the corners of the bag to give the head a more rounded look (see drawing 1).

If you tear the bag by mistake, repair it by pasting paper or tape on the inside.

Crepe paper masks

You can create a colorful, fireproof mask from crepe paper and decorate it with glazed paper cutouts.

It is easier to use just one sheet of crepe paper, but your mask looks more festive if you glue it together from two or three pieces of different colors (see drawing 2). The paper has to be long enough to reach around your head, approximately 30 inches (75 cm.). Drawing 2 is the pattern to follow for the mask on the left in the photo opposite and in drawing 3 on page 54.

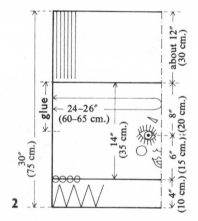

You can turn down the corners of the bag, if you want, and hang tassels, rings and beads to them. You can decorate the mask with small pieces of painted paper or bits of glazed paper. You could even glue on a beard made of yarn.

Measure for eye holes and cut them out.

Make eyes, nose and mouth from glazed paper you cut and glue to the mask. (Notice the eye holes cut through the pupils of the mask in the photograph.) If you want earrings, either cut them out of glazed paper or

When you decorate with paper cutouts, try out new features until you get the effect you like. The eyelashes of this crepe paper charmer are glued on only at one end, so they stand out freely from the mask. The cat's whiskers were made by sticking very thin wires through the cat's nose. To give the effect of ears, this cat pressed together the corners of a paper bag.

*Sad version
of the crepe paper
mask in the photo*

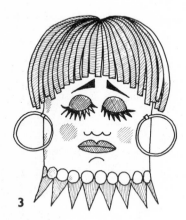

Funny masks

For all of these masks, use cardboard or sturdy paper, construction paper, for example. You can also make them of old cartons or sheets of newspaper glued together. Newspapers make very funny masks, if you use headlines, pictures and text as decoration!

You may want to use the pattern on pages 56 and 57 the first time you make this kind of mask, but next time you'll be able to do without it.

Trace the - - - - pattern onto a piece of paper and cut it out. Then place your tracing on whatever material you are planning to use for the mask—cardboard or paper. Make sure you fold that cardboard or paper in half first, and when you place the pattern on it, be sure that the fold line (· - - - · -) lies on the fold. Then trace the outline onto the cardboard (or paper) and cut the mask through the 2 layers.

Mark off eyes and mouth in the usual way. Cut a nose, too, with a couple of snips of your scissors. You can glue a nose flap over the cut, if you want.

Add some nicks along the bottom edge of the mask. You can glue or staple the nicks over each other so that the mask fits under your chin. See drawing 1.

put on light metal rings with paper strips through slits in the crepe paper. Keep the rings in place on the inside with tape, which also strengthens the mask.

Roll the paper together and cut it into a fringe at the top for hair. Also fringe the bottom edge of the hair. If you want a necklace, as in drawing 3, glue on round pieces of glazed paper to look like beads.

When you have finished decorating your mask, glue it together half-way down the back seam and keep it together over your head with tape or string.

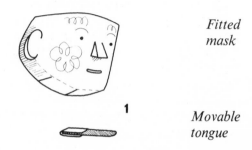

*Fitted
mask*

*Movable
tongue*

It doesn't take much to disguise yourself! This gruesome gang made their masks in minutes. The top hat took a bit longer (see page 72).

Paint or decorate the mask with paper cutouts of glazed paper or glue on some other colored paper. You can add a beard (use black felt, yarn or paper), glasses, a fringe (use paper, see drawing 2), a glued-on nose flap, and even a movable tongue.

Use red cardboard to make the movable tongue, or color it red with a non-toxic crayon. Make it so long that you can hold it in your mouth while you shake it up and down. Cover the part you keep in your mouth with adhesive tape (see drawing 1).

Fringe becomes hair

2

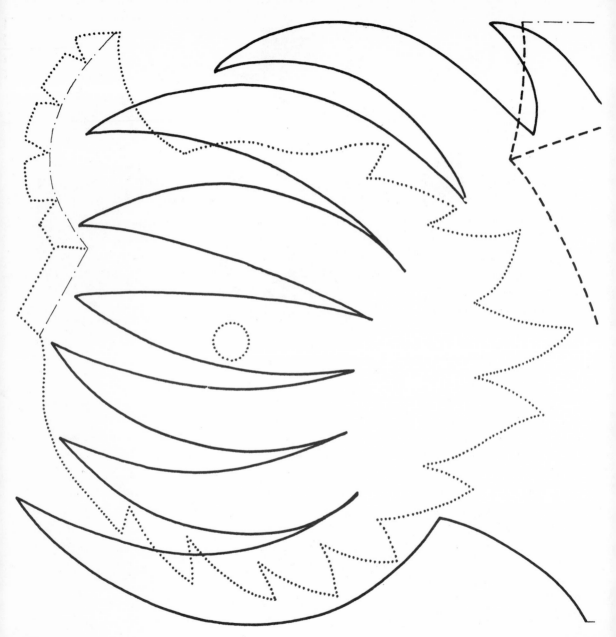

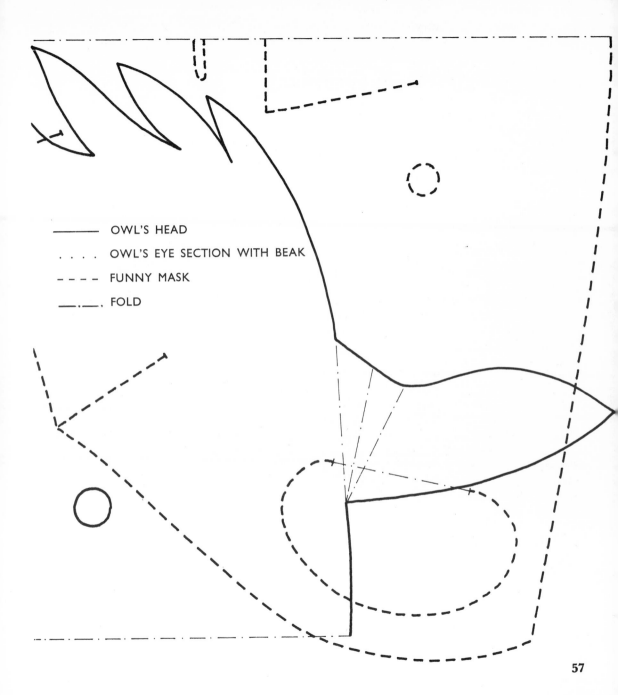

OWL'S HEAD

. . . . OWL'S EYE SECTION WITH BEAK

- - - - FUNNY MASK

—.—. FOLD

7 Total disguises—in cardboard

Bird people

This owl mask is not difficult to make, and you can create many other kinds of birds from the basic pattern.

There are 3 parts to the mask, the actual head, and 2 eye sections with beak.

1. Copy the owl mask pattern (pages 56 and 57) onto tracing paper. Follow the heavy line (——) for the owl's head. You will be cutting both head and eyes double in pieces of folded cardboard (note the location of the fold). Follow the dotted line (· · · ·) when you trace the eye and beak.

2. Now cut out the pattern.

3. You need 2 pieces of cardboard, one dark for the head and a lighter one for the eye sections. Fold the dark piece of cardboard in half and place the owl's head pattern on it so that the fold line (·-·-·-) lies on the fold in the cardboard. Then trace it onto the card-board. Now fold the lighter piece of cardboard and trace the owl's eye section onto it. You don't have to worry about the fold this time.

4. Cut out the head first, then the eye sections. You can use the paper patterns again, if you plan to make more birds. If you want to paint feathers on the owl mask, do it now, before you assemble the mask, but feathers are not essential.

5. Trim off all the points from one of the beaks, as shown in drawing 1. Bend the points of the other beak towards the inside of the mask, cover them with glue, and paste them to the inside of the first beak.

6. Now you have one beak with 2 separate eye sections attached to it. Glue those eye sections over the folded head, so that the eye sections and the beak stick out a little in front of the head (see drawing 2).

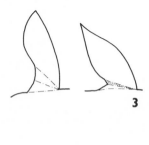

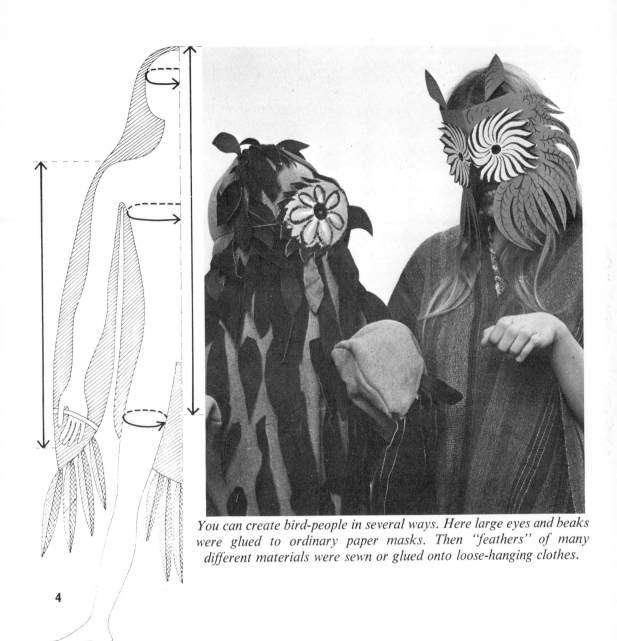

You can create bird-people in several ways. Here large eyes and beaks were glued to ordinary paper masks. Then "feathers" of many different materials were sewn or glued onto loose-hanging clothes.

7. Unfold the mask, lay it flat, and cut out holes for eyes.

8. Bend the horns so that they stand out and forward a little, by folding at the fold lines (· - · · - -, see drawing 3).

9. Finally, keep your mask in place with an elastic band (see page 51 for hints on reinforcing the mask).

Bird costume

For a costume that will suit all kinds of birds, use an old discarded blanket, burlap (hessian) or another inexpensive material. Fold the material in half to make sure it is big enough to reach all the shaded parts shown in drawing 4 on page 59.

To make the costume: drape the folded material over your head. Have someone chalk in a slit for your head on the top of the material. Then take it off and cut the slit. Sew a hook and eye fastener at the back of the neck. Cut two more slits, one on each side, to make sleeves (see drawing 4 on page 59). Sew the cut edges to form the sleeves and the body of the bird.

You could sew real feathers onto the costume, but rags or bits of crepe paper cut out like feathers are just as good. It is easier to sew the feathers on by machine, before you sew the costume together.

Place two straps in the seams inside the tips of the sleeves. They will give you more control when you want to flap your wings.

Cut two holes for the legs with as large a gap between them as possible. Measure for eyes and cut two holes. Place the bird mask over the holes.

Knight in shining helmet

To transform yourself into this crusader from the Dark Ages, you create your own helmet, costume, sword and shield, too. The helmet has a visor which you can lower or raise.

Helmet

Make the helmet of thin, pliable cardboard and cover it with ordinary aluminum foil (kitchen-type). Using silver-colored cardboard saves that step but it won't give such a dazzling effect. Use paper fasteners to put the helmet together (see drawing 4); they look like rivets. The ornaments on the bottom of the helmet are made of gold foil cut double, and the plumes are bright-colored crepe paper.

1. Enlarge the pattern (in drawing 1) onto a piece of paper according to the dimensions shown. (Note that you make the helmet and the visor separately.)

2. Cut out the pattern and check to make sure the helmet is the right size. If not, enlarge or reduce your pattern.

3. Cut out the cardboard parts with scissors.

4. Glue or tape the helmet together and draw the outline of the top (the lid) and another slightly larger than the diameter of the helmet (see drawing 2). Cut around the larger outline.

5. Make notches in the top between the edge and the inner outline, as shown in drawing 3, and bend them down. Make holes as shown in both the helmet and the lid for attaching with paper fasteners. Also make two holes in the visor and two in the helmet for the two paper fasteners which will keep the visor in place. At the same time, prick a small hole for the plumes in the middle of the crown.

6. Glue the aluminum foil over the cardboard. Paste the paper around the edges.

7. Glue on the gold foil and strengthen the lower edge of the helmet (on the inside) with a strip of paper, colored tape or fabric.

8. Use paper fasteners to close the helmet at the top and put the visor on, preferably with a couple of cardboard discs on the inside for reinforcement.

9. For the plumes, cut 3 or 4 double pieces of crepe paper or tissue paper.

10. Glue them together around pieces of wire (drawing 4).

11. Sew the plumes together at the bottom with thread or elastic.

12. Pull the ends of the wire through the hole in the crown with a reinforcing cardboard disc and glue them inside the helmet with paper strips (see drawing 4).

The tunic

In a discarded bed sheet, cut a hole for your head and add a vent in the back, and a button and loop (see drawing 5 on page 62). Sew or iron on crosses or other symbols cut from adhesive-backed paper.

The shield

Select two large pieces of cardboard. They don't have to be very thick, but they should be the same size.

1. Cut them to a point at one end and scrape them with a scissor to create a fold down the middle lengthwise.

2. Glue or staple the cardboards together (see drawing 1 on page 62).

3. Cover the cardboard shield with household-type aluminum foil. Glue the foil on and turn in the edges.

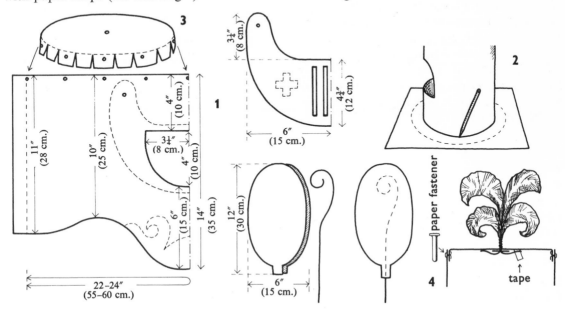

61

4. Cut a cross or some other symbol out of glazed paper and glue it onto the shield.

For a heavier shield, use one thick piece of cardboard, paint it silver, and glue a strip of wood with a small leather strap handle to the back (see drawing 2).

Sword belt

Cut a sword belt from any heavy fabric or from leather. You may want to paint on "precious stones" with a marker, or paste on glass beads. The belt in the photograph is 4 inches (10 cm.) wide. Lace it at the back.

Fashion a scabbard or sword holder (see drawing 3) from leather or the same heavy fabric you used to make the sword belt. Make the scabbard from a "Y" shape. The base of the "Y" is a square 4 inches (10 cm.) on a side. Cut a slit smaller than the full width of the square along a line bisecting (dividing in two) the square. The slit must be large enough to hold the sword but not too large, or your sword will fall through the scabbard. Fold up the square and sew it along the dotted lines shown in drawing 3. Sew or glue the scabbard to the sword belt.

Sword

A strip of plywood acts as your sword. Tack a narrower piece on as a guard, or use 2 short pieces of wood on each side of the handle. Add a cork at the top of the handle for the finishing touch (see drawing 4). Paint the sword. Go over the handle with a strong glue and then wind a string closely around it so that the string sticks to the wood.

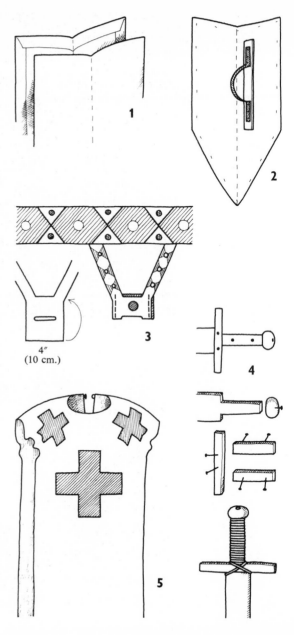

The crusader's helmet and shield are made of cardboard; his tunic is made from an old sheet; his sword is a piece of wood. He is easier to put together than you'd think!

Medicine man

This sorcerer mask is decorated with cutouts of glazed paper and tissue paper. The lower jaw moves.

The mask consists of 3 parts: forehead with hair, the middle piece, and lower jaw with beard.

1. Copy the 3 parts of the pattern from pages 66 and 67 onto tracing paper. Draw the ears a bit larger than those in the pattern: you could make them 4 inches (10 cm.) wide and 12 inches (30 cm.) long, for example.

2. Fold the cardboard in half, making sure that the fold lines (· - · - · -) lie on the fold in the cardboard, and transfer the pattern.

3. Now cut out the mask and long pointed strips for hair and beard.

4. Decorate the pieces with paper cutouts or paint them before you go on to assemble the mask.

5. Glue or staple together the forehead and the middle part (see drawing 1). If you staple them, hide the staples with decorations.

6. Glue the bridge of the nose to the forehead or tape them together on the back of the mask (see drawing 3).

7. Insert an elastic band inside the mask at each side (see page 51).

8. Fasten the lower jaw to the mask with two paper fasteners (see drawing 2), but before you do, reinforce this spot with an extra bit of cardboard (see drawing 3).

9. Tape a strip of cardboard or plastic to the inside of the mask at your lower jaw. It has to be long enough for you to hold it between your lower lip and your tongue (see drawing 3), so that you can move the lower jaw.

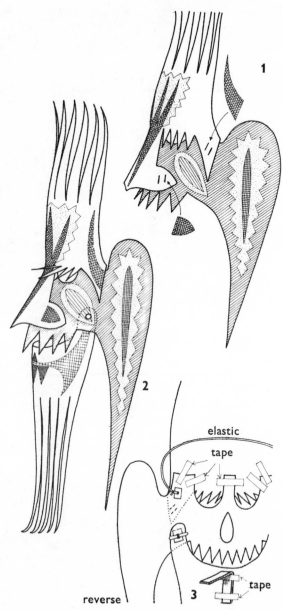

This medicine man moves his mouth when he pronounces magic formulas. Using the same method, you can give other masked characters a chance to move their jaws when they talk.

FOLD—MIDDLE PIECE

FOLD—LOWER JAW WITH BEARD

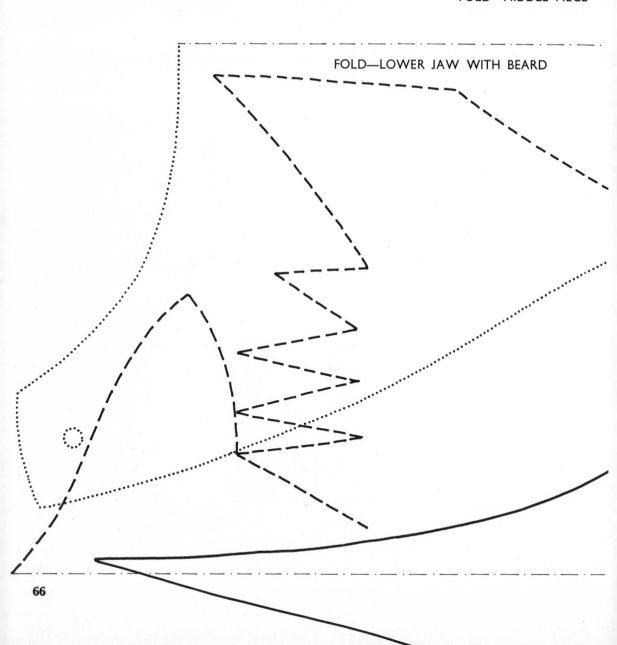

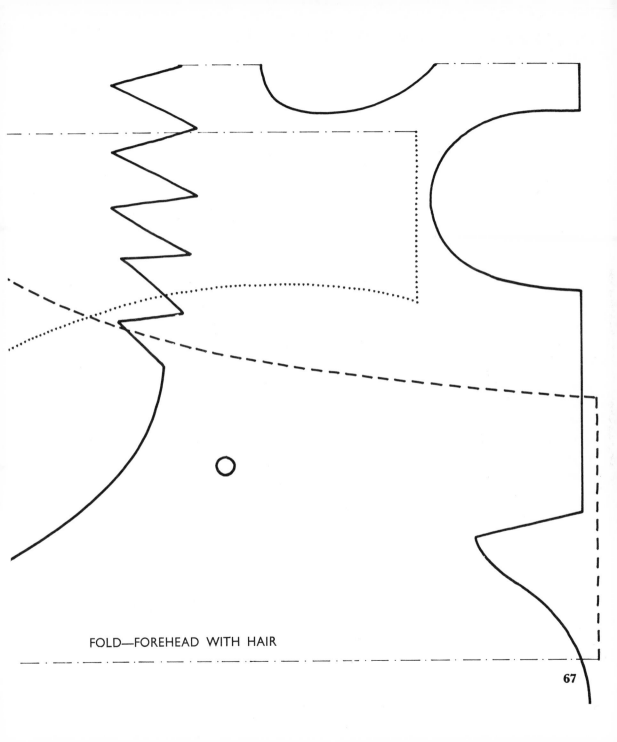

FOLD—FOREHEAD WITH HAIR

This serious elephant is cut from corrugated cardboard with the corrugated part on the inside of the mask so that you can draw and paint on the surface. With a little imagination, and following the same idea, you can populate a jungle, a farm or even a kennel. The elephant is holding a flower made of colored crepe paper and wears a corduroy shirt backwards. Attach a thin tail with a tuft to your costume, if you like.

Corrugated elephant

Corrugated cardboard works particularly well for an elephant mask; it has a rugged coarse-skinned look, but you can use it for many other masks, too.

The "core" of the elephant's head is a solid cardboard ring, around which you build up the mask. The ring fits around your face from down beneath your chin to up and over the top of your head. Make it of regular cardboard which you staple together, or cut it from a carton.

The ring should be 4 to 5 inches (10–12 cm.) wide at the top and approximately 1–2 inches (3–5 cm.) at the bottom. Cut the length to fit around your face. Measure from the top of your head to beneath your chin and back up again (see drawing 1). Hold the ring in place with an elastic band which you staple onto the ring (tie a knot at each end) and which fits around the back of your head.

*You can build
all kinds of full masks
on the cardboard
ring*

Draw a pattern following the diagram in drawing 2. Note that the diagram shows only half the mask, so when you cut it, you must cut through 2 cardboard layers. Be sure to place the fold marks (· - · - · -) on the fold of the cardboard.

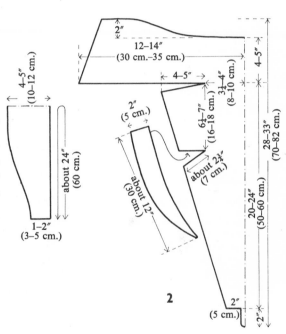

Transfer the pattern to the cardboard and cut it out with scissors. You may need to adjust it a little so that it fits comfortably on the ring.

To staple or glue the elephant's head onto the ring:

1. Staple the crown of the elephant's head to the upper part of the ring (see drawing 3).

Roll the two flaps of the trunk so that they coil towards each other inside the mask. Tape them together on the inside to keep them in place.

Bend the "finger" of the trunk and stick a flower in it.

Paint eyes on the side of the head and cut tiny holes in the front (hide them in a crack of the corrugated cardboard) for you to look through (see drawing 5).

Finally, paint wrinkles on the elephant's forehead and trunk.

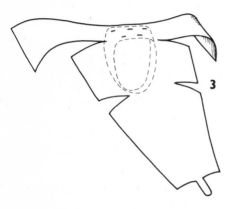

2. As you staple each cheek onto the ring, insert a tusk between cheek and ring (see drawing 4).

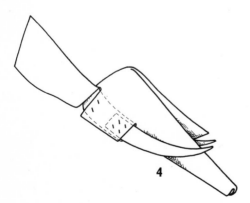

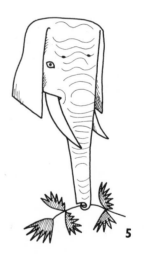

The villain

A full mask is a mask which covers your whole head. The head and hat of this mask are made in one piece.

You make the rolled mask of thin cardboard which you roll into a large cylinder and glue or staple in place.

Head

1. Fit a piece of cardboard around your head and be sure to leave an additional inch and a half (3–4 cm.) for gluing. The thicker the cardboard, the more room you must leave. The cardboard has to be long enough to cover your face and act as a top hat, too.
2. Roll the cardboard into an oval shape and make marks where your nose and ears are. Keep the roll together temporarily with paper clips or a couple of clothespins.
3. Diagrams 1, 2 and 3 all show how to make the villain's nose. Copy the nose pattern in drawing 1 onto tracing paper.

4. Trace your copy onto a piece of cardboard and cut out your new nose.
5. Glue the "x" spots together.
6. Unroll the mask again (it is easier to cut it when it lies flat). Make a T-shaped slit in the cardboard mask (drawing 2), and bend flaps forward on the dotted lines (- - - -).
7. Slip the lower edge of the nose into the slit (match up xx with xx, and xxx with xxx) and glue it onto the back of the cardboard roll. Glue the flaps into the nose (drawing 3).
8. Cut holes for looking through with scissors, while the mask is still lying flat on the table. Cut ears, too. Shape them almost like a half oval and bend them forward.
9. Paint on eyes, ears, mouth, moustache and hair, or use paper cutouts. You can also create hair, moustache and eyebrows from velvet, wool or felt.
10. Now glue the mask together.

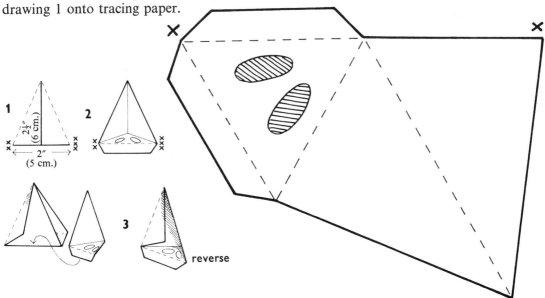

1 2½" (6 cm.) 2" (5 cm.)

2

3 reverse

Top hat

1. Place the mask cylinder upside down on a piece of black cardboard. Trace the outline of the oval (see drawing 4) onto the cardboard. Draw 2 of these ovals. They will be the hat's brim and its crown.

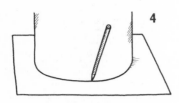

2. Outside the outline of the brim, draw (free-hand) another oval which will be the outer edge of the brim.

3. Cut out the brim—but when you cut the inner circle, leave a little extra cardboard for gluing the brim to the hat. Cut little notches in this gluing-edge (see drawing 5) so that it will go on smoothly.

4. When you cut out the crown, leave extra space on the *outer* edge of the oval and put little notches in it (see drawing 5), and bend them down so that you can glue the crown onto the hat smoothly.

5. Now glue the crown of the hat to the inside of the "roll."

6. Pull the brim down *over* the roll and glue it on.

7. Trim one piece of black cardboard (or paper) to the height of the hat and glue it over the hat so that the notches are hidden.

Putting the top hat together

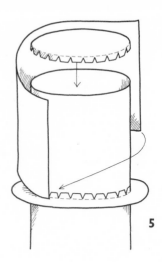

Costume touches

Cut a collar of white cardboard (or paper) about $2\frac{1}{2}$ inches (6 cm.) wide. Glue the collar around the neck of the mask and keep it together in front with a glued-on paper bow.

Finally you may want to trim the lower edge of the mask at the back of the neck and the sides, so that the "head" sits comfortably.

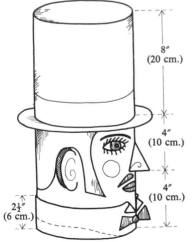

8"
(20 cm.)

4"
(10 cm.)

4"
(10 cm.)

2½"
(6 cm.)

This dangerous fellow with the gun is completely un-recognizable; the mask covers his entire face. Actually, his mask and top hat are made of one long piece of cardboard rolled together and glued or stapled. You can make just his top hat or just his face.

8 Mask tricks with papier-mâché and gauze mâché

You already know how to use gauze mâché (page 22). Papier mâché is done in much the same way and using them both, you can create an endless variety of masks.

Papier mâché consists of pieces of torn paper soaked in paste. Just as with gauze mâché, you glue it over a mould, and as it dries, it hardens. Newspaper is a good material to use; crepe paper gives a finer pulp. Buy the paste in powder form (see page 94) and mix it with water according to the directions on the package.

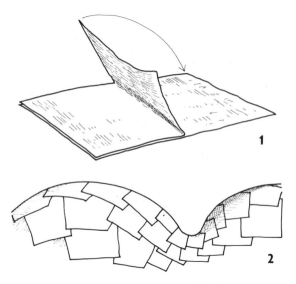

Papier-mâché technique

1. Apply an even layer of paste to a sheet of newspaper.

2. Put a dry sheet on top and press them together. It is a good idea to fold the dry sheet together in the middle and put it on halfway, while you smooth the rest of the sheet from the middle outwards.

3. Tear the double sheet into strips and divide the strips into pieces.

4. Glue the pieces onto your mould, large pieces on large, even surfaces, small pieces at tricky spots where there is detail or a sharp curve (see drawing 2). Every time you add a scrap of paper, paste it on with your glue-brush (see page 75); stroke every piece from the middle out, overlapping them like shingles. You need to apply two to three layers of paper scraps to make a solid mask. It is easier to paint the mask if you paste down a sheet of white, absorbent paper as your final outer layer.

Using the half mask you've created, take measurements for eyes and nose and cut holes in the mask for them. You cover the nose hole with a "bump" from an egg carton. Cut it crooked, so that it becomes a snub nose. Glue the "bump" over the hole. Cut a hole in the "bump" for breathing.

If you don't want to use the egg-carton-bump nose, use half of a red ball (trim it a little so that it doesn't pinch the bridge of your nose). Keep it in place with a thin elastic around your head.

Paint the mask and give it hair and moustache. Remnants of fur were used in the photograph on page 76.

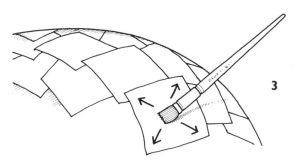

3

5. Let the mask dry completely before you paint it. Drying time depends on the thickness of the layers, but figure that you need to let it dry overnight.

6. Use the same kind of paint (poster paint) that you use for paper masks. When the paint dries, it looks dull. Varnish will perk it up.

For a large, sturdy mask, combine the two materials—papier-mâché strips and gauze.

Balloon masks

Modern clown

Following the directions for papier mâché (page 74), use a balloon as your mould. Measure it as you blow it up so that you stop when it corresponds to the size of your head. Cover the balloon with papier mâché strips just a little bit more than halfway down the balloon. Let it dry overnight.

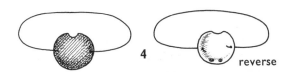

4   reverse

*Bald head
with ball
nose*

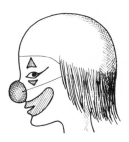

If you have trouble keeping the mask in place, put an elastic band from ear to ear and down behind the back of your neck, as in the drawing on page 22.

Clowns are needed—for parties and games and plays as well as for circuses! These modern clown masks are made of papier mâché and gauze mâché (the derby too, see page 30), moulded over a blown-up balloon. The noses are bumps from an egg carton. To make the bald head, see page 22.

Ghouls and girls and mâché masks

Apply papier mâché or gauze mâché to a balloon. Completely cover it and then cut through it lengthwise and you have two masks. If you don't want to use a balloon, you can use a round or oval-shaped bowl, a plastic container, even a large bottle. You can mould a nose over almost anything, a small bottle, a piece of folded tin or any other odds and ends. Cut the nose to size with a scissors when it is dry.

Witch

This ferocious and arrogant witch has a pointed nose and pointed chin, both made of paper cones.

Mâché mask possibilities are endless! The witch on the left pokes her paper-cone-nose and chin into everything. The phantom is very sinister; it can even rattle its teeth! Who knows how the country girl got into such company, but her bangs and braids are made of twine.

Make a full papier-mâché mask and take measurements for eyes and nose. Draw circles on the mask to indicate where to place the cones. Shape a long and a short cone of cardboard. Cut them slantwise so they'll fit the mask. Apply a couple of layers of papier mâché. Cut holes in the mask, where you have marked off for the nose and the chin (see drawing). Glue the ends on inside the mask. You may strengthen the cones with a little more papier mâché where they attach to the mask.

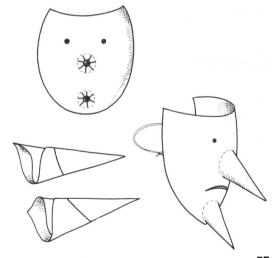

Paint the witch any way you want, but remember that the bolder her features the better they will show up from a distance. Finally, insert an elastic band in the mask (see page 51).

Skull

Use the balloon method to shape the skull. Then trim it around the back of the neck, up above the ears, and down to the lower jaw. Cut teeth in it, so that they protrude and look horrifying.

Make the lower jaw separately out of thin cardboard and attach it to the skull with paper fasteners. Now insert a mouthpiece (see page 64 for the method to use), and you will be able to rattle your lower jaw.

Paint the skull white or very pale yellow with black eye sockets.

If you wear a dark sweater, preferably one with a turtle neck so that you can get it to cover your ears, and a dark sweat suit (or tights), the effect is gruesome! A large dark cape or coat pulled up around your ears is frightening, too.

Country girl

The balloon shape suits this ravishing rural wench. Her nose is a cardboard cone or the bump from an egg carton. To make it stick, cut it so that a little of the carton is left on. Then put it through a hole in the mask and glue the wide part on the inside of the mask.

Give the girl rosy cheeks and large blue eyes; a wig with braids will make her complete (see page 21). The braid in the photograph is made of yellow twine.

Use an elastic band to keep the mask in place (see page 51).

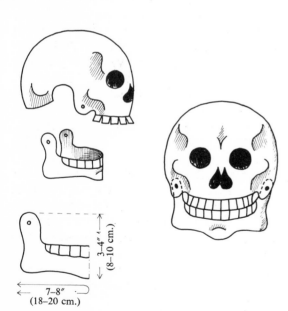

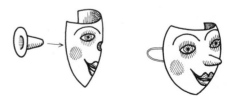

The two-person horse

If you want to make a giant-size mask, like a horse's head, you need a fairly solid frame over which to build it. You can use chicken wire, steel wire, or reeds (the same kind you'd use for basket weaving). Giant masks generally rest on your shoulders.

This horse's head is for a two-person horse. You mould it over chicken wire which you cover with a mixture of papier mâché and gauze mâché.

The frame, which you shape in your hand, is constructed in two parts—head and neck. Eventually, you will attach them to each other.

1. Shape the wire frame neck to fit the measurements of the person who is going to be the front end of the horse. Leave plenty of room for the head. Loop the chicken wire only as far as the chin (see drawing 1).

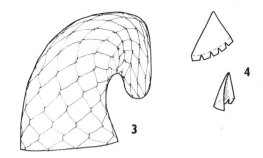

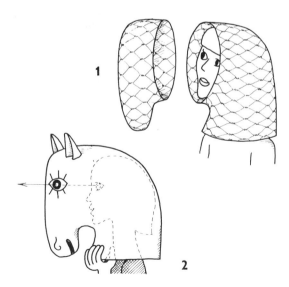

2. Shape the horse's head, fit it to the neck, and sew it to the wire (see drawing 2).

There are several ways to create a frame. You can buy wire netting in one piece and bend and shape it (see drawing 3). In some spots you'll need to clip it with a wire-cutter and then bind it together with a little more wire to get the shape you want. As you shape the horse's head, try to get the eye holes lined up with the place where the painted eyes will be (see drawing 2).

3. Cover the structure. The first layer is of papier mâché (see page 74). You don't have to tear the double pieces of newspaper into very small pieces, especially not when you're covering the neck. Be sure the papier-mâché strips cover the lower edge thoroughly. You also need to papier-mâché the inside so that you don't scratch yourself on loose ends of wire.

4. On top of the layer of paper, apply one or two layers of glued gauze pieces. This makes the head more solid.

5. Make the ears of thin, tough cardboard or stiff leather. Cut notches in them for the gluing operation (see drawing 4). It is a good

79

idea to reinforce the spot where they join the head by gluing gauze mâché pieces on top of it.

6. Paint the horse's head a color that matches the material you're using for its body. You can get a dappled effect by painting spots on both head and body, if you like.

7. Paint eyes and poke holes through the pupils for looking through. If you weren't lucky enough to get the horse's eyes in just the right spot so you can see through them, make a couple of holes wherever you need them. If you paint the horse a dark color, you won't be able to see the "extra" eyes.

8. The horse in the photograph has a mane made of yarn. You can wind the yarn around a piece of cardboard, cut it as shown in drawing 5, and sew it onto the cardboard a little distance from the edge with back stitches and then glue it onto the horse. You could also use unravelled burlap (hessian), straw, excelsior or wood shavings for the mane.

Headpiece

You can put together a glamorous headpiece for the horse from scraps of leather or cloth. The headpiece of a circus horse might have plumes on it (see drawing 6 and page 61).

6

7

8

9

Horse's mane

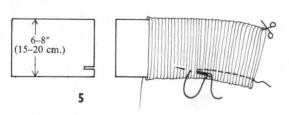

6–8″
(15–20 cm.)

5

Body

You can make the horse's body from burlap (hessian) or discarded blankets or sheets.

Simply fold over a single sheet or piece of burlap and sew together the front and rear edges only. Leave an opening for the head and a tiny one for the tail (see drawing 7).

Inside the horse

The person in front wears the head and holds it on. The person in back should be the taller of the two. He or she should hold onto the belt of the person in front. If the person in back wears a belt, you can attach a tail of yarn (same color as the mane) to it. Stick the tail through the top corner of the rear seam (see drawing 9). This tail serves a double purpose: it keeps the blanket in place while it moves in a lively way. You can sew the tail onto the blanket instead, if you prefer.

You can make other giant masks using the same method. Instead of its resting on your shoulders, though, you might want to make the large head come down over your chest and back (drawing 10), or you might create one that sits on the top of your head and ties under your chin (see drawing 11).

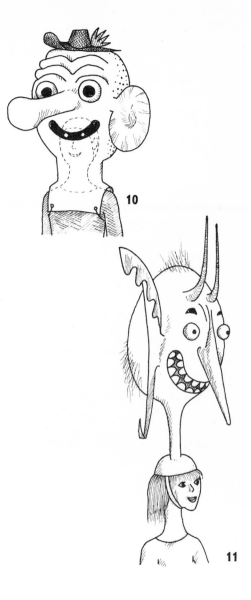

This very friendly horse is partial to sugar. When he starts to dance, you'd never guess that he's made of paper, gauze and chicken wire!

When you shape papier mâché over clay, you can use the same mould many times. This one was inspired by a Greenland exorcist mask. Can you imagine it coming at you across the ice?

The exorcist—Greenland style

Using papier mâché or gauze mâché over a clay mould, you can create striking masks. Make the clay mould of plasticine (see page 94) or plaster of Paris.

To economize on clay, use an oval bowl or a brick as a base for your modelling (see drawing 1). Apply the clay in small lumps until the mould is the shape and size you want. Measure the mould against your face to make sure it is the right size. It should reach all the way around your face to your ears.

Smooth the clay with a stick or a knife (see drawing 2). Make the mould high; with large features; otherwise, the finished mask will seem flat.

3

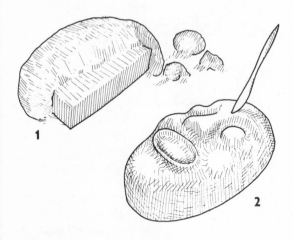

1

2

When the mould is ready, spread petroleum jelly over it to help you to remove the papier-mâché mask easily.

Cover the mould with papier mâché (page 74) or gauze mâché (page 22), cut out whatever air holes you need and let it dry overnight.

When the mask is dry, trim it at the edge, and cut it at the hairline. Strengthen the inner edge with tape or an extra layer of papier mâché, and insert an elastic band (see page 51). Your exorcist could wear a parka or a cloak on which you attach rags, bits of paper (crepe paper is good) and strange string objects. You also need a magician's wand (see drawing 3).

9 Masks of wood, cloth, string and foil

Masks on a stick

Masks that attach to a stick have many stage uses. In a matter of seconds, you can become another person. In fact, you can play two parts at the same time!

A mask on a stick doesn't break easily, and you can use it dozens of times without having to adjust it—the size fits all heads!

Lollipop masks

Call them lollipops because they have the stick in the middle. Use them for star, sun and flower masks, which you can paint or sprinkle with sparkles. Moisten the surface with paste or glue diluted in water and stick the sparkles on.

Double stick masks

This type has a painted face on each side, maybe the same person—happy on one side, angry on the other—and you turn the mask according to your mood. Place the stick to one side of this mask, and you'll always know which side is out: happy—right hand, angry—left.

The sides can also represent two different people. Then you can hold a conversation with yourself. Naturally, you use two different voices.

A lollipop mask—with sparkles. Cut it out of cardboard or saw it out of plywood. Sparkles come in many colors (silver and gold, too) and they stick easily onto damp glue.

Half mask on a stick

Even if a stick mask hides only your eyes, it can create surprising effects.

All of these masks are two-faced. The laughing one on the left covers almost the whole head, but on the back it has a cross face with droopy mouth. The middle mask leaves the lower part of the face free. On one side it reveals an old king with metal foil crown and steel wool hair. The other side is a young wooly-haired prince. The mask with the glamorous eyes covers only a small part of the girl's face, but it makes a strong impression. Turn it—to find out what she's really like!

To make a stick mask:

1. Create your own paper pattern on newspaper and make sure it will fit your face.

2. Draw the mask on cardboard, plywood or Masonite and allow a little extra space at one side for attaching to the stick.

3. Cut or saw the mask.

4. Saw a small groove in a round stick.

5. Place the mask in the groove and attach with staples (see drawing 1).

Back to bag masks

It is simple to make a cloth mask in the shape of a bag; it fits snugly, and it won't break easily. You can decorate it with all sorts of trimmings—either glue or sew them on.

To make the bag mask: Cut a piece of cloth long enough to reach from your neck over your head and down to your neck in the back, as shown in drawing 1. Pin the sides together so that it covers your whole face.

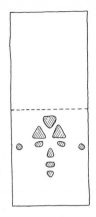 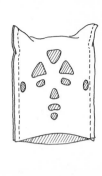

Feel your way to where the holes for your eyes should be and mark their position with chalk.

It is easier to put on the trimmings before you sew the bag. You can glue on bits of felt or appliqué them (see drawing 2); you can sew on straw or raffia (see drawing 3); you can attach rings and beads with a thread and needle (see drawing 4).

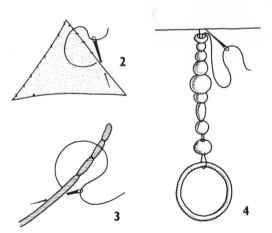

You can pull your own hair through the holes in a bag mask, as the girl on the left did, or let straw braids stick out. The mask on the right is made of black silk, the hair is white cotton yarn. It is trimmed with embroidery, beads and colored buttons.

The hair in the photographed mask on the right shows a center part. The ends disappear in the seam. Add a couple of beads and a knot to the tips of the long strands of straw. You can sew on more and longer pieces, too. The weight of the beads keeps the straw in place, and besides, they are fun to dangle. This kind of straw trimming can practically serve as a costume by itself.

If you want the mask to stand out, away from your neck, fold back the lower edge of the mask and make a "casing" with a piece of wire inside it. For a round-headed look, pull an elastic through the casing.
If you don't want to have to sew so many different things to your bag, don't do it. You can go a long way without a needle. Glue on large eyes, a nose, a silly mouth, and put on a funny hat instead of fussing with hair (see drawing 5).

5

You might cut holes in your bag and pull strands of your own hair through them. It's easy to do and a funny idea.

Anything is possible when you decorate this kind of mask. Use your imagination. Something delightful is bound to happen!

String masks

You can create a witch doctor's mask and other exotic-looking masks from string or thin rope, straw, and a small piece of felt or cardboard.

As you see in the photograph on page 90, the mask on the right is made of tough string which is rolled into spirals to form circles or ovals with a hole in the middle. There are two eye rings, one ring for the mouth, and two rings forming the cheeks.

1. Start by rolling up the string for the eye rings.
2. Staple together each circular turn, unless you'd rather sew them together, which makes the mask look neater. Roll the eye rings large enough, approximately $3\frac{1}{2}$ inches (9 cm.) in diameter, so that you can look out easily through the center holes when the rings are sewn or stapled together.
3. You need more string for the cheeks. Make a test coiling when you are ready to roll them up. Start rolling and keep on until the cheek rings meet the eye rings (see drawing 1).

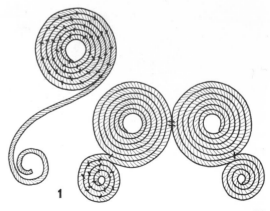

1

These masks of straw and string look exotic even though they are made of the simplest materials. The mask on the left is a big bundle of straw which has been cut in the middle. The whole bundle was sewn onto a half mask, and cardboard tubes (from rolls of toilet paper) were stuck on for protruding binocular eyes.

4. Roll a larger oval for the mouth. In the photographed mask it is about 4 inches (10 cm.) wide and 6 inches (15 cm.) long.

5. When you've finished rolling and securing the string coils, sew or staple all five rings together so that they do not unravel (see drawing 2).

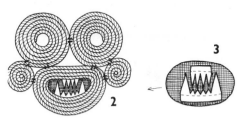

6. Cut the teeth out of white cardboard. Glue them onto the back of the mouth opening (see drawing 3). Behind the teeth, glue a piece of black or red felt or cardboard.

7. Cut a half mask of felt or some other material long enough to reach from ear to ear, and approximately 3 inches (8 cm.) wide (see drawing 4).

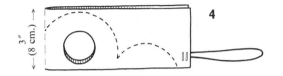

8. Mark off the eyes and cut them out.

9. Gather up the straw in small bundles and staple it to the half mask.

10. Join the string mask and the half mask by stapling or sewing in such a way that the half mask is completely covered.

11. Fasten an elastic band to the lower edges of the half mask.

12. You may want to put a straw beard under your chin, and perhaps add a few beads? They may be magical!

Fantasy masks from metal foil

If you want to make a fantasy mask, thick metal foil is your medium. It comes in silver, gold, and colors, and you can buy it from crafts suppliers. You can use cardboard, too, and perhaps a combination of the two is best of all.

For an angelic creature, you may want to use gold or silver foil. A mixture of foil and red cardboard is perfect for a traditional fiend (don't forget the horns). But you'll want to go further than that.

Before you give free rein to your imagination, make a half mask which fits your head really well. You'll be attaching the metal strips to this half mask.

1. Cut the half mask out of thick cardboard, being careful to place the fold lines (· - · - · -) of your pattern on the fold of the cardboard.

2. Measure and cut out holes for nose and eyes (see drawing 1). Also measure the mask to make sure it fits from ear to ear.

3. Bend the ends of the mask and glue them together, inserting elastics that fit around your ears. Then staple (see drawing 2).

4. To avoid wasting metal foil, cut a pattern for the strips. Fold it in the middle. Then you can draw strips and cut them out double. Many of the most attractive masks are symmetrical, but cut your strips any way you like. Drawing 3 shows some examples, but with this type of mask, especially, there are no rules.

5. Glue or staple the strips together. One strip might stick out and bend so that it forms a nose.

6. Decorate the mask with bits of glazed paper, colored streamers, beads strung on wire—anything you choose!

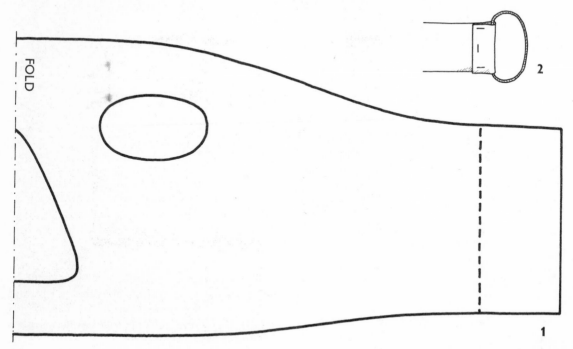

FOLD

1

2

fold   **3**

*This fantasy mask,
cut out of colored
metal foil, gleams
when light shines on
it. If you don't want
to buy metal foil,
use colored cardboard
—or combine
cardboard and foil.*

10 Supplies—what to get and where to get it

Crepe hair: A braid made of artificial hair, crepe hair is used for false beards, moustaches, and eyebrows. It is available at shops that sell grease paint.

Epoxy: A strong glue, it is excellent for gluing on glass ornaments and gluing metals together. Follow the instructions on the package carefully. The glue may irritate your skin. You can buy it at hardware dealers'.

Foil: Metal foil is available from crafts suppliers in several thicknesses; buy a sheet the thickness of a postcard. You can get copper foil (red), brass foil (yellow) and aluminum foil (white). It is easiest to work with the copper.

Aluminum foil used in the kitchen is too light for most masks: use it only when it is specified.

Gauze: Regular surgical gauze is available in several different weaves; and the close-woven is best for gauze mâché. A large roll measures about half an inch (1 cm.) by 18 inches (45 cm.). Buy it from drug stores.

Grease paint sticks: Many brands are available; see supplier list.

Leotard: An elastic garment used for gymnastics and ballet, available in several colors from some hosiery shops and costumers.

Nose putty: Available from shops that sell grease paint, it is a soft wax that you shape with your fingers.

Paste: Available from art supply and hardware dealers as powder or flakes which dissolve in water.

Plasticine: A modelling wax available from crafts suppliers or art suppliers.

Poster paint: Tempera or acrylic paint; available in tubes from art suppliers.

Soft-tip markers: Markers are excellent for painting on cardboard and other materials, but not recommended for use on your skin. The color is difficult to remove, and some people are allergic to them.

Spangles: Available loose for sewing on costumes or already sewn on long tapes which you attach to the costume. Available at fabric and yarn shops.

Sparkles: Available at variety shops.

Spirit gum: An adhesive for sticking on false beards and moustaches. Purchase it from shops that sell stage make-up.

Stain: A preparation for painting wood, available from paint and hardware dealers. Water-base stain dyes materials well, but the color is not fast on cotton.

Straw: Straw can be purchased in bundles from garden shops and florists; in colors from crafts suppliers.

Synthetic resin glue: A white glue for hobbyists and woodworkers (Elmer's is a synthetic resin glue), it can be used with plastic foam and many other materials.

make-up

In the U.S.A.

Look in the yellow pages under Theatrical Make-up, Theatrical Costumers or Equipment. Local dealers are listed there. If you cannot find any in your area, you can write to any of the following manufacturers and distributors, who will send you a free catalogue:

Bob Kelly Cosmetics
151 West 46 Street
New York, N.Y. 10017

Marco Bergmann Co., Inc.
(Leichner make-up)
599 11th Avenue
New York, N.Y. 10036

Stein's Theatrical Make-up
430 Broome Street
New York, N.Y. 10013

Stores that sell make-up outside mainland U.S.A.

Dooley's Fun Shoppe
208 West 5th
Anchorage, Alaska

Attco
2855 Koapaka Street
Honolulu, Hawaii

In Canada

Makeup Center
904 Sherbrooke St.
Montreal, P.Q.

Masq Shop
1034 Dundas St.
London, Ontario

Robinson Plays
47 Simco Street
Toronto, Ontario

Sun Specialty Co.
10143 112th St.
Edmonton, Alberta

In England

A. H. Ltd.
146 Lower Road
London S.E. 16206

Charles Fox Ltd.
25 Shelton Street
London W.C.2.

Selfridge's Ltd.
Oxford Street
London W.1

In Australia

Seveides Pty. Ltd.
Queen St.
Brisbane Arcade
Brisbane, Queensland 4000

In the Far East

Nippon Stein's Co.
Copu Ebisu #517
10–14 Ebisu-Minami 3-chome
Shibuya-ku, Tokyo, 150-00
Japan

Oriental Trading Co. Ltd.
7 Aguilar Street
Hong Kong

wigs and costumes

The following theatrical suppliers publish catalogues which are often free to schools and organizations. Write them for further information:

American Scenic Co.
P.O. Box 283
Greenville, S.C. 29602

Atlanta Costume
2089 Monroe Drive N.E.
Atlanta, Ga. 30324

California Costume
15976 E. Fracisquito
La Puente, Calif. 91744

New York Costume Company, Inc.
27 West Hubbard Street
Chicago, Ill. 60610

Northwestern Costume
3203 N. Highway 100
Minneapolis, Minn. 55422

Rubie's Costume Co., Inc.
86–15 Jamaica Ave.
Woodhaven, N.Y. 11421

INDEX